The Nature Constellations Handbook: An Invitation to Connection

Re-membering Nature in Systems

By Francesca Mason Boring

First Published in the United States in 2022 by
All My Relations Press, Evans, Washington
www.allmyrelationsconstellations.com
Black and White Interior Version ISBN: 979-8-218-03064-3

Cover photo by: John Crum

Dedication

This book is dedicated to my parents, grandparents, uncles and aunts, siblings, cousins, husband, and ancestors who all had influence in my intimacy with natural world. I honor all the lands that the blood of my ancestors have come from. I have been abundantly blessed with indigenous teachers and elders.

Carrying the blood of indigenous people, from my mother's side (the Newe/Shoshone) from lands in the United States that have topsoil and ground filled with the memory of my family, and being descendent on my father's side from refuges from Lithuania and immigrants from Scotland and Ireland, I feel the echo and importance of place in my bones.

With respect for the foundation and support from my bloodlines, it is also incumbent upon me to express gratitude for the miracle of two women who have influenced and encouraged my work in systems constellation and specifically nature constellations.

Sneh Victoria Schnabel of Freiburg, Germany, was my first teacher in Family Constellation. She was a generous and challenging instructor. She exuded precision, and expert facilitation of what was then, and still is, an emerging methodology. Having been among the first generation to sit with Bert Hellinger, Sneh was fearless in placing representatives for rivers as easily as she placed representatives for human parents.

An artist, and consummate student of human relationships she has an extraordinary ability to look at herbs and human beings with open curiosity and an appreciation of what they might bring forth, given the right combinations. Having a graceful relationship with spirituality and respect for diverse cultures and family histories, Sneh has been a living example of the powerful ramifications of trust.

Anngywn St. Just introduced herself to me first through her book: Relative Balance in an Unstable World: A Search for New Models for Trauma Education and Recovery (2006).

Sharing her original introduction to trauma therapy utilizing the natural world, writing openly about her familial proximity to war, I found her background in art history, medicine and her exchange with Bert Hellinger alive in her work. As I had the good fortune to have personal exchange with her, I continued to be encouraged by her clarity and humor.

Anngwyn's acceptance of indigenous healing traditions and her unique ability to be inclusive of those American historical realities, which are often ignored or hidden has been heartening. Her integrated approach to including the impact of 'greater forces' on human kind and individuals has invigorated my commitment to invite the land to speak.

We are a part of the earth. It could be no other way. I honor these, and the women in my life who have embodied deep relationship with Mother Earth.

In addition to dedicating this book to these two extraordinary women, there are two other innovators in the work to whom I would like to extend my appreciation.

I am grateful to Tanja Meyburgh, of South Africa, Co-founder of **R**esources for **E**mbodied and **A**ncestral **L**earning (REAL Academy) for allowing the inclusion in this text of some of the materials which are included in the On-line Nature Constellation Course which allowed the presentation of Nature Constellations for a wider audience.

My thanks also to Barbara Morgan, from England, Editor, The Knowing Field (the international English language journal on Systemic Constellations Work), who has given permission to include various excerpts, and some articles I have written which were included in the journal over the years on the developments in Nature Constellations.

To my cousin/brother, John Crum, Shoshone, I appreciate the permission to share your photograph of the landscape on the Duck Valley Indian Reservation on the cover of this book. May it nurture others as much as it has nurtured me.

In my heart, as I write this book, there are so many who stand behind me, have mentored me, loved me, stimulated and motivated me, and my hope is that they are felt and smile as you explore these pages.

For all indigenous people, story is medicine, history, entertainment, a balm for the collective soul of the community, a gathering for humor and healing.

Nature Constellation is one of the treasures which I believe holds the potential to help us understand and celebrate the story of the integral relationship of human kind to our natural world.

I honor the generous facilitators who have made the time to contribute to this text. May every seed be kissed by the sun.

Table of Contents

Invitation to the Journey

Welcome. You are in the right place. Whether you have been one of the many souls feeling isolated and alone, or one of those who has a sense that you are to be a catalyst for shining a light on the illusion of isolation, this is a book that will provide tools that may effectively expand your resources and honor your resilience.

This book will provide specific tools for facilitators of systems constellation, but it is designed to broaden options and interventions for teachers, therapists, parents, partners and human beings who are tired of a way of perceiving the world which is compressed, petty and destructive.

You may find your own way; perhaps you are drawn to read the book from front to back, or back to front or you may simply allow yourself to pick and choose what you read and when. Accumulatively, all of the parts contribute to the whole, a whole which is pragmatic and encouraging.

The image that continually provided support for the emergence of this text was one of a mountain meadow. Meadows, particularly in the spring and early summer are rich with variety. The number of flowers that may be found are varied, the grasses, the surrounding foliage, the rich soil, alive with worms and millions of creatures we cannot see who are busy holding up the earth, nothing has to be an exact duplicate of anything else. There is a peace in breathing in the complex aroma, and if our gaze softens, we can take in the whole. This does not change that no two flowers are the same. Some of the same species are varied in color, some may hug the ground while others reach for the bees.

In listening to what was unfolding I have felt compelled to honor the contributions for the flowers that they are. Some of the contributions in this book are from areas where the Queen's English is the normal written language, and the contributions of other writers are presented with the spelling that is standard for their region.

There are writers from other countries who have a syntax which is slightly different, and still, has perfect rhythm and content. I honor the distinctions in the same way I do not expect a lupin to bloom like a daisy, or carry the aroma of an apple blossom. I invite you to enjoy the subtle differences of the presentations.

The chapters are provided by seasoned facilitators who model the kind of humility and curiosity that can mentor your wading into an expansion of your work and world view. They are generous human beings who face the chasm of not knowing what will emerge, trusting that we will have the courage to integrate something new. Whether or not you venture further into including nature to a greater degree in your life and work, my conviction is that these voices will embolden and encourage you.

Included in the book are nature constellation meditations. One of the meditations invites a deep process, particularly relevant for those who experience anxiety in regard to environmental issues. In every case, nothing needs to be rushed, and you can pause, or explore another avenue for a moment if you are not ready. These meditations are ways to engage groups, or to support yourself in exploring the deep sense of our participation in the natural system, to remember that we are a part, we are connected.

There are examples of nature constellations, templates for constellations that facilitators may employ, and descriptions of systemic constellation experiences through which nature opened a door to deeper understanding, a new openness, and peace. These have wide application.

Some of the chapters are shared in the form of story. They are non-linear embodied invitations to 'feel' nature in systemic constellations and to inhale the way of learning that is our natural inheritance.

In addition to the chapters there are contributions that are like seeds in the soil, or plants about to burst into bloom. These are delicate insights and sharing by numerous facilitators which I hope will serve as a pollinator for those who hesitate to step forward in isolation.

May you be strengthened by this work and these voices as you remembered your birthright of kinship to Mother Earth.

The Emergence of Nature Constellations

Nature Constellations materialized in the field of Systems Constellation, which originally emerged as Family Systems Constellation, brought to the world by Bert Hellinger, formed by a matrix of influences, not least of which were the Zulu people and the indigenous paradigms and rituals of South Africa.

Family and systems constellation utilizes the placement of representative of members of a system to 'map' the system. Through representative perception, representatives experience a 'knowing' about their position within the system- emotions, reactions to other participants, occasionally statements or verbiage which is surprisingly accurate in representation of what that part of the system actually experiences.

Through observing the mapping, innate knowing, and the coherence of the knowing field hidden dynamics which have been problematic within a system may be understood in a new light.

It may be that even Hellinger did not acknowledge that he was directly influenced by the Zulu, but I wanted to share those places where there is distinct parallel:

- The importance of primacy, or hierarchy in the system (again this is something that used to be fundamental in many wisdom traditions and cultures)
- There is a healing modality, utilized by Zulu and others, which involved throwing bones. In that healing ceremony, the bones are thrown, the mapping that is evident in the placement (by the field) of the bones, is observed by the healer (Sangoma) and there may be recommended changes or identification of which ancestor is hindering well-being. The Sangoma will often give the client a "healing sentence". This can have the structure of a riddle, or poem, but it is something to take with, to allow the healing movement to continue.
- Honoring destiny is a fiber in the weave of Zulu culture. I heard a story about Hellinger asking why the people were not angry with their parents. The response was, "They gave me my life. What I do with it is my responsibility".
- As many other indigenous cultures, reciprocity was fundamental in Zulu tradition. The balance of give and take was organic and an important fiber of the community.

Each of these are elements which are foundational in family & systems constellation, developed by Bert Hellinger, who spent 16+ years with the Zulu people.

There is a depth of inference in being fluent in a particular language. There are transmissions in idioms, inflection and sharing. Hellinger spoke German, (his mother tongue) and English, and Hellinger spoke Zulu. It is difficult to imagine that he did not have access to a deeper knowing of the people than those who opted not to go that extra mile to learn the language. In addition to speaking Zulu, I cannot help but think that Hellinger must have taken a deep dive into the culture because he was working with the people during the ecumenical movement in the Catholic church. This was a time when the doors blew off and there was a spirit of inclusion and inquiry that may have been unprecedented in the Church. In addition, having walked the grounds of one of the monasteries where Hellinger worked and lived in South Africa, I could not help but notice the proliferation of Zulu regalia, and ceremonial items that were present there.

I cannot say that Hellinger's development of constellation work was influenced by the Zulu people definitively, but I can say that many of the aspects of the work were present in the Zulu culture hundreds of years in advance of family constellation work, as many of the elements were present in numerous wisdom traditions throughout the world. When I honor the work, innovation and courage of Bert Hellinger, I also bow to the many cultures and customs which far preceded this modality, often times having elements of caution and humility that is almost foreign to linear thinking.

When I work with indigenous peoples from the Americas, and elsewhere, or even with people of Asian descent, I often acknowledge what is: that many cultures in the past were very aware of these essentials, particularly connection and 'field' phenomena which modernity had mocked as 'spooky' or superstition.

I was reminded of Hellinger's openness, and flexibility when I heard Alexander Shi, from China, give a presentation at the International Family/Systemic Constellation Conference on-line (May 7-13, 2022) which was translated from Chinese. During his lecture Shi shared Hellinger's proclamation in China that this work was simply an expression of the Tao. Hellinger was open to cultural influences and there are cases, when without fanfare, my impression was that he organically included cultural elements which were part of the system.

Family Systems Constellation is a formidable approach which allows individuals to conceptualize hidden systemic dynamics which have injured their family system, relationships and personal well-being. The modality may contain structure (in a constructivist approach) and may also engage in the 'knowing field', this landscape through which understanding emerges by inviting the 'big picture'. This emergence of insight, statements, movements which represent actual dynamics within systems (family systems, organizational systems, communal systems, natural/environmental systems) is a demonstration of what is referred to as a phenomenological approach.

In 2003, the Constellation Conference in Würzburg, Germany invited me to present a workshop: Mother Earth Belongs. This was a presentation which allowed me to introduce the concept of including Nature in systemic constellations, including family constellations. One of the handful of participants who attended was Berchtold Wasser, a forester from Switzerland. Berchtold eventually developed the first year-long training in Nature Constellations. At the same conference Berchtold was joined by a number of parties at the same conference in an Open Space, which invited discussions of varied issues. The Sixth Sense in Service was a group which emerged from the discussion in that forum. The group included: Berchtold Wasser, Chrisjan Leermaker, Joannes Schucker, Christine Robert, Erna Alexandra Jansen, and Kenneth Sloan. For more than a decade, together these facilitators explored the systemic field of nature and the implications of our human interface within that system.

In 2013 Returning to Membership in Earth Community: Systemic Constellations with Nature was published, Mason-Boring, F. & Sloan, K. (2013). The book had contributions representing various aspects of Nature Constellations illustrated in chapters written by a number of pioneers in this essential application of systems constellation work:

Sneh Victoria Schnabel, Germany
Daan van Kampenhout, Netherlands
Berthold Wasser, Switzerland
Zita Cox, England
Beth Murray & Peter Devries, United States
Sarah Fancy, United States
Chrisjan Leermakers, Netherlands
John Cheney, United States
Andreas Demmel, Germany
Kenneth Edwin Sloan, United States
Susan Scholsser, United States

Since the time of the publication of the Systemic Constellations with Nature book there have been many innovations in nature constellation. We have more facilitators including nature in their way of working, acknowledging it as a resource, and articulating aspects of this approach which are helpful for facilitators of constellation work and other modalities, as well as supportive of humans and our cousins and brothers and sisters in the natural world.

Perhaps one of the most encouraging results of experiencing Nature Constellation is that participants, groups, and communities may experience an embodied sense of the combination of reciprocity and responsibility (Wall-Kimmerer, R. 2013) which was understood by our ancestors, before modernity, before the separation of science and soul, before the dogma of autonomy and the resultant sense of isolation and disconnection.

Introducing and including nature in our systemic world-view, allows a rich reconnection to what sustains us. And, if we are to believe what is experienced by many in Nature Constellations, and the growing body of research regarding the sensate nature of nature, much as family constellations reconnect those who have been separated from the systems that resulted in their physical birth, we are able to expand the felt-sense of a belonging which dispels the illusion of painful isolation by supporting the reconnection of human beings to the natural world.

Seeds:

Initially it wasn't easy to integrate nature into my work. I had to ask for help and was guided by the online course work. Now, after some years, I can perceive more deeply -it feels like an iceberg melting; a work in progress.

The rewards of including nature in constellations have helped me relax in my work. I often ask if the client has a favorite tree they would like to bring into the constellation for support. Each time I have been surprised by the love between human and tree. One person shared that they sit under a certain large tree that reminds them of their grandfather when facing some difficulty.

In one community/nature constellation a representative for a native tree experienced a great openhearted kindness toward a non-native or exotic breed tree, something that gently reflected the opposite of a human polemic here and everywhere.

I'm deeply grateful for nature herself

-Tanya Shapiro, LMHC, Family Constellation Facilitator, Argentina

tpshapiro@gmail.com

instagram @buen.lugar.constelaciones

What can Nature do for me?

We are essentially drawn to nature as a resource, comprised of a sentient community of peers, the natural world is a consummate healer of isolation and loneliness.

In western modernity, there is a proliferation of the posture in which value is based upon, "What's in it for me?" What can nature actually *do* for me?

Although we have a deeper resonance with Mother Earth in our DNA, it is fair to address the pragmatic relationship with forces and elements in nature that are now well researched.

We are at a lovely apex. There are currently volumes of experiential 'knowing' coupled with research that indicates that we are excluding the consciousness and generosity of nature at our peril.

But this may be just a symptom of what Amitav Ghosh refers to as the great derangement. (2016) In Ghosh's book, the Great Derangement he points to our literature, history and politics as being active forces in distracting us from realities regarding our impact on the world. The illusion of our separation has become collective, and we continue in this ignis fatuus to our detriment.

For practitioners and persons who fear being ostracized or not taken seriously when stepping deeper into relationship with nature and becoming aware of our systemic symbiosis, it may be grounding to become aware of how many indicators are now established that remind us that if we continue to be confused by our delusions of separation, we forego actual benefits.

Earthing, aka Grounding, is a simple age-old tool that allows individuals to reconnect to the ground, but in addition, appears to have a powerful impact on the body. (Wilson, D. 2019) What is involved in this powerful tool? Simply walking with bare feet on the ground. Within minutes, in a measurable way, standing with our feet on the ground appears to restore the internal bioelectrical environment for the normal functioning of all body systems.

The Japanese practice of shinrin yoku, or Forest Bathing, has numerous physical benefits which are outlined by Dr. Qing Li (2018). Li's research indicates that simply being present to the trees in a forest can impact stress levels, blood pressure, immune system function, creativity, mood, and even the health of one's cardiovascular system, to name just a few of the benefits he verified through research.

We now know that gardening does in fact nurture happiness. This feeling of well being is actually due in part to the activation of microbes in the soil that stimulates the production of serotonin. (Tenenboum, L. 2020)

Research in Finland indicated that when children were regularly interacting in greenspace, by digging and playing outdoors in a rich natural environment, soil microbes also seemed to increase the diversity of intestinal microbiota and the research indicated an increased T-cells as well as other immune markers in the children who were encouraged to interact with the earth (Cassella, C. 2020).

Numerous research projects to date indicate that developing green spaces decreases violence in urban neighborhoods. (Bowen-Gernstein, D. and Williams C., 2020). Engaging community in the planning, development and nurturing of parks, community gardens and green gathering places has additional measurable benefits.

The inclusion of Nature in architectural design and construction is helping us move closer toward physical and emotional health. Bringing light and plants into a building uplift the spirits of those who work and live in a space, but there are also physical impacts. Vitamin D deficiencies have risen as civilization has moved further away from the sun, bringing light into a building through informed design can help to decrease the fatigue and depression which can accompany the vitamin deficiency which can result from a lack of sunlight (Chavan, T., 2021). Plants, in addition to creating a lovely environment can be included in design as a component of air filtration and food production.

What is most encouraging for constellation work is that an introduction to these exchanges with nature is possible though the representative perception experienced in a constellation when individuals stand as representatives to allow greater understanding of any system.

For those who are discouraged thinking nothing is changing on the environmental justice horizon it is good to look at the strides that are being made in the arena of Environmental Personhood, which is the argument that nature herself has intrinsic rights and warrants the same protection and legal identity afforded to any human being:

- New Zealand's Whanganui River now has the same legal rights as humans- recognized by the courts as having personhood.

- Bangladesh became the first country to grant all of its rivers the same legal status as humans in 2019
- Yurok tribe in the United States recognized the rights of the Klamath River pursuant to the tribe's traditional kin relationship to nature
- In the Philippines the Supreme Court accepted litigation on behalf of future generations.
- Bolivia and Ecuador have enshrined the rights of nature in their constitutions
- Environmental personhood has been recognized for Asia's Ganges River

These designations are not written in stone. Daily, indigenous people and environmental justice interests are involved in attempting to widen the legal recognition of the primacy and dignity of nature, and sadly there are occasions in which some efforts have been overturned by higher courts. In 2019 voters in Toledo, Ohio passed the Lake Erie Bill of Rights. Unfortunately, in 2020 a federal judge struck this protection down, declaring it was unconstitutional for a litany of reasons.

With international, collective expansion of our awareness of our 'right' place in the world, it stands to reason that there is a great possibility that the recognition of legal identity of nature and natural elements will continue to expand, both in legislative efforts and within our human consciousness. This expanding global recognition of the 'personhood' of land is not new. This awareness of our interdependence, respect, even love, is written in our DNA. This is not to deny that some of our ancestors and the land had an adversarial existence with the natural world, but as human beings our beginnings were based in awe and the reality of our limitations. This interdependence, this reverence, may not be a criterion for scientific research or linear observation. But, our souls, our human systems can easily re-member the gratitude for the rain, the hope of the rising sun, and the inherent healing in the quiet of a starlit night.

Family Systems Constellation reminds us that each of us belong. We come from a family, we all have ancestors, every one of us has a place. Nature constellation is the natural extension of understanding that just as we all come from 'someone'...our family systems have come from 'somewhere'.

We are living testimony to generations of courage and cowardice, each leading to the survival of our bloodline. We are a testament to the resilience of human beings and the generosity of the natural world.

Our human interface with endless wars were historically shared by horses, donkeys, mules, dogs, camels, elephants, carrier pigeons, dolphins, and other creatures which were enlisted to support combat (2015, Elgan). It is rare to find a child's history book which includes the exploits or the significance of these compatriots in our military history.

Canines and geese have protected humans for centuries, warning when strangers approached and instinctively protecting their charges and their shared territory with a vengeance.

The bones of the ancestors are in the land. Nature has challenged and nurtured us, and all cultures and countries have a history of originally being connected to the land.

Family Constellation work is often described as helping us re-member...those parts of our families that have been excluded and forgotten; the system insists that they all belong to us, as we belong to them.

Nature Constellation has the potential to bring about the deep peace one feels when they embody the sense of being 'at home'. When we begin to acknowledge and re-member the earth as our home, we have the potential to personify the balance that comes from standing with our feet on the ground, feeling the immensity of the sky and the mountains. We re-member the systemic gratitude that comes from the truth that the earth has cared for our families for millennia.

In addition to supporting our sense of wholeness, this approach provides tremendous potential in the arena of helping us to understand the environmental systemic challenges. Working with companies, NGO's, entrepreneurs, neighborhoods, farms, pets, horticulture, forestry, botany, and a host of other disciplines provides nearly limitless potential markets for this work.

When family constellation work (ala Bert Hellinger) came onto the world stage, it provided a needed and often welcome lift for many in the therapeutic communities. My hope is that for those who are facing the systemic stress on natural systems, Nature Constellations will provide much needed relief and new paradigms which elevate the discussions and provide both innovations and sustainable interventions.

This sense of vision is fueled by your courageous commitment to this journey. It is sunrise in this aspect of systems constellation. I wish for you many bright days walking with Nature Constellations and the relief of a systemic philosophy which supports human beings and our Mother Earth.

Seeds:

Nature has a voice

It was a hot July day in Southern California, about 30 people had gathered outdoors at a local park for a Nature Constellation workshop. I had already been a part of many Constellation workshops but this was my first time at one dedicated to nature.

There is so much that has stuck with me from that day but there is one constellation that had a very profound impact on me. The issue holder was from out of state and part of an environmental group concerned that the local mining would pollute the local water with uranium.

From our circle people were chosen to represent. As the constellation unfolded a possible resolution came up in the constellation creating a more relaxed field.

But, and here is the part that really stuck with me, the representative for the water made the statement "uranium is a natural part of me, what is stressing me is all of the anger and fighting among you (humans)". Why is this what so stands out for me? There was never a thought to treat the water itself as a sentient being with knowledge of what it did or did not need or want. And herein lies what I feel is one of the major gifts of nature constellations, a way to not only ask nature but to open to the possibility that what I, what we humans, think is harmful or helpful may be very different from how nature sees it. Nature has a voice and Constellations help us to listen.

Nancy Kehr, D.C., USA

Can individuals be impacted by events in nature which have been significant for ancestors?

There have been times when there have been natural disasters such as floods, tornadoes, hurricanes, volcanic eruptions, and even more prolonged natural catastrophes such as drought.

When families have faced forced migration due to military conflict, we are more apt to be aware of those greater forces. Being somewhat separated from nature at so many levels, many of these cataclysms which may have resulted in mass deaths in a family or community due to natural forces, such as weather events are often excluded from our family narrative.

The American Dust Bowl was a significant disaster in the 1930's in which a combination of drought, and poor land management resulted in one of the largest migrations in U.S. history. Over tilling, a lack of soil conservation practices, displacement of native plants such as deep-rooted prairie grasses, followed by draught, massive dust-storms created food insecurity and resulted in mass migrations, economic disturbance, death, disease and family separations.

This specific historical period reverberates in numerous family fields. In constellations which include these natural catastrophes we are not only able to honor those traumas which still echo within the bones of living descendants, but we are able to embody an understanding of the deleterious impact of Manifest Destiny, the idea we have a God given right to claim and dominate the land, even to the point of destruction of our natural resources.

Some family systems have been strongly impacted by exploitation of the land. Unethical mining practices which poisoned resources or led to mining disasters may impact the descendants of those who profited from the extraction process which put miners in danger.

We often forget context of these events. Many mines were worked by extended families, sometimes whole communities migrated to foreign lands or areas for work. Children would often accompany the miners, carrying lunches or actually laboring, crawling into the smaller spaces in the tunnels that adults could not access.

When mining accidents occurred, it was not unusual that the children, uncles, fathers, spouses, within one family would be trapped, lost, or buried within the mass grave of a mine collapse. The sense of being disoriented, having difficulty breathing, fear of darkness, are all phenomena that may systemically follow a family for generations. When such discomforts are without explanation in one's own life, and when there is persistent oppressive experience of terror and even specific fears that echo the historical event, it is not irresponsible to open up a line of inquiry regarding events in the family history that may elucidate the presence of such a present distress when there seems to be no other rational for such discomforting symptoms.

Deforestation is another land related exploitation that may have long term impact for perpetrators as well as those who are displaced by the industrial razing of a land. In some cases, the destruction of forest or jungle lands may be intended to displace or starve out residents. The impact of the destruction of flora and fauna has collective impact beyond that immediate populace that is targeted. Our modern inability to perceive events in a wholistic way has had environmental impact and human cost beyond measure.

Thinking systemically, with families who are not currently involved in exploitive industry, it is not unusual to trace generational loss back several generations to times in other centuries when populations were pushed out, or starved out, by alteration of the land or other natural resources.

This has not always been a standard line of inquiry to advance healing and collective consciousness. We have a unique opportunity to include Nature and the natural world in the conversation when we are trying to identify the point of origin of an individual's pain or confusion.

Seeds:

'Throughout my experiences with trauma, it has become increasingly clear that Nature offers those in healing and helping professions, a valuable cross- culturally available resource for understanding and healing trauma.. Nature offers all forms of healers, healers and their clients many lessons in devastation and renewal.

Beyond devastation, our natural world offers a wealth of healing resources. One can find a life history of a tree, for example, according to the pattern of its rings, or find a map in the shell of an oyster, which tells the story of its life and relationship to the sea. I have come to believe that we are rather all like tree rings and oyster shell patterns in that what happens to us leaves a permanent record. The goal of trauma recovery, therefore, as I see it, is not to erase or to cure but rather to expand to include and grow larger than whatever has happened to us. If one thinks in terms of integration and of resolving rather than eliminating trauma, then there is a possibility of guiding a multi-dimensional human organism toward an experience of relative balance and resiliency."

Relative Balance, Anngwyn St. Just (St. Just, A., 2018)
Anngwyn St. Just, PhD
http://www.acst-international.com

Group Exercise: What did your parents teach you about nature?

Have the group break into dyads.

In introduction to this process, it is important to indicate that this exploration will be precisely timed. Each question will be given exactly 5 minutes for response. If there is open space, and one has no answer or little to say, both participants within the dyad will sit in silence until the next question is offered.

Following the format used in a previously developed interchange The Schism of Ism, which was presented in The Knowing Field, Issue 38, June 2021, the two participants will have opportunity to share the following exchange.

One asks the other, one person in the pair asking each of the questions, the other in the dyad is the respondent:

What did your father teach you about nature?

The other speaks, uninterrupted for 5 minutes. If the speaker is finished in 3 minutes, the two sit in silence until the second question.

After 5 minutes (carefully timed) the one asks the other:

What did your mother teach you about nature?

The other responds for up to 5 minutes to that question.

When the 5 minutes has passed, the partners in the exercise switch and the second person then has the opportunity to respond to the same two questions, within the same monitored time frame of 5 minutes.

This exercise can lead to the wonderful realization that one's love for nature was actually learned from an early age, mentored by parents who were connected or excited by aspects of the natural world.

It can also be the case that one's fear of nature is understood in new light as the cautions and reactions of one's parents are brought into focus.

Learning 'nothing' about nature from one's parents is also a teaching.

After the dyads have completed it can be helpful to open the group to a short debrief if there is something that participants feel strongly to share. This can expand the perspective of the participants beyond their own experience.

There are times when these questions open an understanding of systemic influences, historical or familial events that colored the stories and attitude of parents, and the relationship of the family line to the natural world.

Most salient after this exploration was the sharing of one participant who stated, "I only now realized how much I am teaching my children, or not teaching my children about nature. My participation in this conversation for the future of my children and my descendants will be changed."

Personal Reflection for Facilitators: What did your parents teach you about Nature?

When facilitating Nature Constellations, or in working to integrate a holistic, systemic perspective regarding your relationship to the natural world, this line of questioning is not restricted to a group activity.

Before evaluating your own beliefs, your own anxieties, your own intensions and impact in regard to creation, it is helpful to first really discover, what have you inherited?

What did your mother teach you about nature?

What did your father teach you about nature?

Without judgment or agenda, allow yourself to experience the answers to those two questions. What is the field of your family system in regard to nature?

One of the most touching insights that a participant of this inquiry shared with me was that it fostered a realization that the next generation would be inheriting a systemic perspective regarding nature. As a parent, as a teacher, we are instructing younger charges what nature is, what our relationship to her is, whether the natural world is a safe place or to be feared. This review of the unconscious systemic perspective gave birth to a rich and relevant question:

What am I teaching the children about nature?

When we are conscious of our 'inherited' system, we are in a position to evaluate objectively whether our paradigms serve. Are our beliefs in fact, in service of a healthy interconnection, or are they an unconscious deterrent to our being able to celebrate our alliance and bond?

Constellation Exploration: The Hollow Bone

In this moment I would invite you to consider the deepest level of service in systems constellation. And, in the context of Nature Constellation, when we are considering the earth, the relationship of human beings to the planet and all the living beings of the earth, and conversely their connection and relationship to us, it is important to consider that we are able to hold that investigation with such integrity that we cannot but call it sacred.

We often have human representatives stand to represent different aspects of a system. It is also possible to place objects as representatives, still demonstrating visible indicators of relationships or barriers.

The representative perception that occurs for each of the people standing as a representative is a powerful phenomenon. Through the spatial representation of those who are standing, or the felt sense that is experienced by those who are willing to stand in the place of some aspect of the system, various dynamics in the system are revealed, there is a 'mapping' which becomes visible. This visible mapping that emerges in a constellation process can bring about a greater understanding of a system as a whole, or insights regarding the interplay of various components of a system.

Occasionally facilitators and participants may feel overwhelmed by the intensity of a representation in a constellation. The indigenous tradition of the 'hollow bone' and knowledge of theory/ techniques on the part of the facilitator can greatly minimize/prevent any residual discomfort on the part of participants of systems constellation. For the collective field of facilitators and participants it is important that those tools, facts and theory which safely support representation in constellation be understood by facilitators.

To represent in a systemic constellation, and to facilitate, one of the stances that is supportive is cultivation of becoming a 'hollow bone'. This is a descriptive term sometimes used in some Native American spiritual traditions which refers to being available to serve and being able to maintain an emptiness that is free of personal agenda or dramatics.

In many meditative traditions, there is a similar instruction. To hold a position of mindfulness, to be open to observing in a way that is clear and clean is something that can be developed and opens the possibility of being able to be present for another, without judgement.

In nature constellations, as with constellations which serve to remove perceived barriers to flow, it is important to leave one's own bias, and personal conclusions out of the process of being in service by representation. In the case of environmental issues, if one feels hysterical, or weakened by emotion, it is important not to stand as a representative while immersed in a personal paradigm that would prevent a completely new perspective from emerging.

Summary Cautions regarding representation:

Announce that anyone can, and should decline to be a representative if they have any hesitation about standing in a role.

It is best if the representatives do not know each other well.

Avoid having people from the same system standing as representatives (wives, siblings, children, parents). Although there are some who have done a great deal of work and they may have stood in many constellations, there have been instances when a dynamic in a constellation agitated what had originally been a relatively benign tension. It is not always possible, but if representations in which there is a powerful dynamic can be represented by people who do not have deep personal bonds, it removes any possibility that their own conflicts would bleed into the constellation. Moreover, if a client, or those present who would benefit from the constellation suspect a bias due to their perception that the actual personal relationship between representatives has priority over their representation, it is in service of the experience of transparency and certain neutrality, and even more of a surprise when deep connection reveals itself in a constellation if those standing in a constellation do not already have established bonds and relationship.

For facilitators and for those who are willing to represent, be aware of the body- we only need information, we do not need anyone to suffer or be physically uncomfortable for an extended period of time. Encourage representatives to relax their body if they are in a challenging physical stance.

People are responsible to de-role. If you are willing to stand as a helper you have to be strong enough to stand, not a distraction from the process. If you are fragile in the moment, overly tired, have any judgment about the subject or the client/ seeker – do not stand

Remember to Check with the representative when representation is difficult:

"Is this too much? You do not have to stay in this pain, if something changes, be aware and let me know.

Be aware if a representative begins to maintain a physical stance that is unfamiliar to their body for a long period of time, the human body can experience muscle strain, or there can be a deeper level of exhaustion than necessary when someone stands too long in a position that is physically awkward.

Encourage representatives to simply stay with the body-what is happening in the body.

Caution representatives to avoid making conclusions/ interpretation/or lecturing when representing

- Representatives:
- The hollow bone (an open conduit)
- Ego (wanting to control the constellation)
- Self
- Self as Facilitator

Wisdom traditions utilized 'the knowing field' for millennia. This 'knowing field' is most evident in constellations is in 'representation'. For facilitators, representation is often not understood or introduced in the context of mechanisms and facts regarding representation in a constellation.

German research documented the efficacy of representation in constellations; neuro-research indicates that the hippocampus identifies the world in spatial mapping (Sanders, L. 2016); quantum physics implies the revelations in constellation through representation as a likely, natural phenomena.

There are a variety of tools for facilitators and participants to minimize any residual difficulty that might occur from standing as a representative in a difficult role.

There are special challenges in modern western society. Healing models in the west wrestle with a 'dependency' on the part of 'patient's/clients', practitioners being surrogate parents and 'responsible' for the care, health and wellness of clients.

Indigenous traditions assume a level of responsibility when one participates in a healing circle. In many wisdom traditions one should decline to participate if one is not well, or 'clean'. Self-evaluation of the representative is indicated before standing as a representative in many healing traditions. Do I have permission?

There are techniques to 'de-roll' but this workshop addresses a deeper level of what being a representative requires, what the responsibilities are when facilitating and standing as a representative, to contribute to the 'knowing field' in a good way.

TALKING CIRCLES:

When there have been collective epiphanies in a group, or when there has been a dynamic which is very painful, when something has impacted the whole of the group and it does not feel that the majority in the group have feeling that they can easily integrate, it is possible to invite a talking circle.

A talking circle, in an indigenous sense, is not a platform for debate. This is a coming together, again, moved from a sacred place, not motivated by the limitations of cognitive competitions. There are times when it is necessary to give that clarification before having participants move into talking circles, or one large talking circle.

It is important for the facilitator to give an introduction of Circle Technology: Each person speaks, no grand-standing, listen, no critique, sharing what is present in the 'field' in the moment: (Outline protocol for talking circles- talking circles as a way of understanding and honoring 'the knowing field')

Small Group Break Out: with instruction that there needs to be a recorder for the group.

Question for each group: What are the challenges of representing, what difficulties have been encountered?

All Constellations are the beginning of a movement not a stagnant solution.

After each small group has made a round to state challenges regarding representation time will be given for the recorder to speak to their small group what the talking points for the group are- to be presented for everyone.

The recorder for each group will state for the whole group what the issues are that participants have encountered with representation in constellations.

Summary Ritual: Honoring the family destinies we are privileged to represent; honoring that we will commit to leaving the representation after we have served.

Sacred Representation:

There is a responsibility for the facilitator and representatives in relationship to the integrity of the sacred service of representation.

Friend do it this way-that is,
Whatever you do in life,
Do the very best you can
With both your heart and mind.

When one sits in the Hoop of the People,
One must be responsible because
All of Creation is related.
And whatever we do effects everything in the universe.
-Teachings of White Calf Buffalo Woman (Lakota)

One area of difficulty for facilitators and participants is the representation of a person or element in a constellation.

Looking at an individual family system dynamic, an organizational system, or a larger collective field, the safety of participants is the commitment of a responsible facilitator.

Portions of this chapter are included in, Sacred Representation, The Knowing Field, Issue 30, June 2017

Constellation Exploration: My family system and nature

When there is a group, or an individual who feels a need to explore their relationship to nature, or if perhaps one feels unable to connect and is unsure of the reason for the hesitation, it can be helpful to explore the dynamic in a constellation.

Place a representative for:

Nature

My Father

My Mother

This provides one level of exploration. Added to that constellation, or in lieu of, representatives can be placed for:

Nature:

Maternal Grandmother

Maternal Grandfather

Paternal Grandmother

Paternal Grandfather

After exploring the relationship of those in one's family system to Nature, it is helpful to place a representative for the client. It may be that you are moved to encourage the client to place just representatives for:

Nature
Self

It may feel appropriate to place the representative for the client as an addition to the family of origin, to see the completion of the relationship of the 'system' to nature.

When we are facilitating Nature Constellations, or when we are providing a constellation for someone who has angst regarding environmental crisis, it is incumbent upon us to be as clean as possible.

My anxiety, intentions, agenda, and systemic traumas should not be a deterrent to a client having access to an opportunity to see what wants to unfold for them to have greater clarity regarding their question.

Of course, washing ourselves before being in service as a facilitator is an ongoing process and something which has been encouraged through the ages in a variety of disciplines.

Facilitating Nature Constellations Outdoors

One of the ways in which a facilitator can increase the interface with systemic constellations and nature is to offer a Nature Constellation Workshop, or several days of training outdoors. In offering an outdoor platform there are several things which can be helpful. Make no mistake, some of these observations and suggestions came through trial and error. My hope is that others do not need to make the same errors that I made, originally assuming that the field would take care of everything- forgetting that I was responsible for attention to specific details which would support a solid container for the work.

First, the location is important. If the constellations are going to include family constellations it is important that the location be a private space. If a family system is working through issues such as sexual assault or other sensitive issues which have been hidden for generations, it is important that the client and the representatives feel sheltered. If the group is outdoors in a public space, privacy is not guaranteed.

Conversely, if the constellations are related only to nature, and do not involve issues which would be consider confidential, it is of real benefit to secure a public space outdoors. Parks, campus grounds, and other spaces which have foot traffic can actually be a benefit, both for the growth of the work and the field.

One suggestion, if the constellation gathering is outdoors in public, is to define the field in a way that makes the working (constellation) space distinct. This can be done with flagger tape. This is a plastic tape that can be purchased at hardware stores and it tends to be made in neon colors, it is sometimes used to demark property boundaries, or tied to oversized loads to encourage other drivers to pay attention. You can secure the tape indicating the boundary of 'the field' using tent stakes to secure them. This creates a border that it is visible from some distance- visibly indicating that there is an area that is demarked. If you are in a public space, one of the goals is to expose new people to nature constellations. For the curious, who are unfamiliar with the work, it is not unusual for someone to physically venture into the constellation space to hear better or to get a closer look. When the area is clearly marked, it can provide a space that is more secure, and allows those who are unfamiliar with the work to observe without breeching protocols that are unknown to them.

Another thing that has been helpful is to have a small handout available. Facilitator Trainees, or those familiar with the work can have an open eye for those who are venturing into the group out of curiosity. Many small announcements can be printed on a single piece of paper. Normally, having a nice graphic also makes the small handout warm and encourages an experience of hospitality. The following is one of the short texts that I have used when a training group is having a constellation meeting in a public place:

Welcome to Nature/Environmental Systems Constellation, adapted from the Family constellation Work of Bert Hellinger.

You are welcome to observe. Thank you for not disturbing this process. This group is currently training in Systems Constellation.

For more info: Coordinator contact info

Website information:

As an aside, the field is in play in every aspect of the work. In one case, a man who was walking his dog came over, received the welcoming handout and began an exchange with the facilitator who gave him the document. He had actually been searching for a place to do constellations, had read several things about the work and was eager to be informed about local resources and events.

Shade is important, and adequate restroom facilities are important.

Remember to inquire regarding permits. Many public spaces need to be reserved and there may be fees for the municipalities in which the park is located; the public space may also require some payment or temporary business license. Due diligence is important and can help you prevent any inconvenience or disruption of the group.

Another consideration: acoustics are very different outdoors than they are indoors. Initially I rejected the idea of a sound system, but I found that if the group was large and the Circle was outdoors, it could be very difficult for the client to hear the representatives when they spoke. Some individuals do not project well, and without a sound system they are not able to speak loudly enough to be heard.

When few people in the Circle could hear, but the statements that the representatives were making were powerful and relevant, it was easy to observe the frustration growing in the group.

For the facilitator, if the group is meeting for several days in succession, there may be real physical irritation for the throat, a microphone can help project one's voice for that amount of time without physical strain.

If the group is small, the sound is not as much an issue as the Circle can be much smaller. But if a sound system is needed, based on the recommendation of one seasoned facilitator who is also a musician, a wireless microphone is preferable. If there is a microphone that has a wire running to the speaker, it can be a tripping hazard, and a definite distraction. In addition, it is advisable to obtain a sound system that has more than one rechargeable battery. Many speaker/microphone systems do not have batteries that will last for the duration of a full day workshop. Having two batteries charged at the beginning of each day allows a workshop flow without interruption.

In Nature Constellation Facilitation trainings one of the exercises that is helpful is to invite the group of facilitators to break into dyads outdoors to experience in an embodied way the limits of sound when facilitating outside.

In advance of the group stepping out to practice, inform the facilitators that in this experience, one will be the speaker (or facilitator) and the other will be the listener. Encourage the couples to spend some time, first with one facilitator speaking to the other, gradually backing up further and further away from their partner (the listener). It is good to encourage the participants to actually tune into their body and be very aware of the level of effort required to be heard clearly by their partner. Invite them to test various positions and distances; what is required of the facilitators body and voice to be heard if their back is to the listener? The listener can continually give feedback to the one who is speaking- to let them know how well they are heard.

You may set a time and invite that the participants switch so that each person has opportunity to be the listener. Each has opportunity to be the facilitator.

Occasionally there is surprise at learning what it actually would take for one to be heard clearly outdoors without a microphone.

There are some basic cautions regarding facilitation outdoors that some might assume would be a given, but it is important to remember that not all who are drawn to experiencing constellation work outdoors have experience being outside on a regular or extended basis. In fact, part of the beauty of offering an outdoor workshop is that for some it is perceived as a safe and interesting platform through which they can be introduced to being in a natural environment.

Our body is a part of nature. Just as an informed respect for the natural environment has sometimes not yet been learned, respect for the limitations and needs of the human body has sometimes not yet been an integral part of life's learning.

As a facilitator it is advised that you take care to provide information that may not be innate for some of your participants. Sending out an email, or providing a handout before the outdoor gathering can be helpful.

Be prepared with a small first aid kit.

Encouraging personal responsibility is important. This is an opportunity to reinforce the level of consciousness and attention that participants will need to hold throughout the nature constellations.

Some of the things that you want to be aware of, and your participants should be reminded of are:

- Cautions regarding weather. If the weather is hot, or unseasonably cold, it is good to advise participants that they may need to dress with layers, perhaps bring a blanket if there is a bit of wind, wear good comfortable shoes.
- Bring a hat and sunscreen. If participants are in the sun for any length of time it is important that they are prepared to prevent sunburn.
- It is important to stay hydrated. You may advise participants that it is good to bring a thermos with water. This may be especially important if you are in a location without faucets, and if you have to walk a bit and it is not possible to pack in enough water to provide it for the whole group.
- If there are bee allergies, it is important to remind folks to bring their epi pin, or mosquito repellant if they are historically a favorite on the mosquito menu.
- If you are in an area which has a prevalence of Lyme disease you may want to provide encouragement for folks to dress for tick prevention as well as check for ticks after the workshop. In some areas emergency rooms routinely give a prophylactic dose of penicillin if someone has been bitten by a tick.
- Another aspect of safety is a quick reminder that there is no refrigeration, so care should be given in the foods that one brings and the preparations they make.

Many of these suggestions sound obvious. But, if fortune prevails and you are actually opening a new door for folks who have not recently spent time outdoors, or who never make the time to spend a day outdoors, it is a good precaution to be sure that people have been informed in a way that allows them to have a safe and expansive experience.

Seeds:

The trees and bushes outside my office often play a part in constellations as seen through windows. They have brought qualities of weathering storms, strength, rootedness, home for birds, pleasurable color, etc. Though they pretty much are always in the same position, suddenly at the appropriate moments, the client's eye is drawn to them and they clearly become representatives in the constellation, enriching the message and expanding the field. It's not uncommon that following this, clients feel more connected to their nature siblings and this provides additional support.

One structure I use with a group or individual is to hold a question or intention in mind then, go out in nature, noticing where you're drawn. As you approach a being (which could be any of the previously mentioned beings or as "simple" as a spider web, moss or a pile of decaying leaves), honor their presence and ask permission to ask your question. Offer something in gratitude (tobacco, a strand of hair, corn meal, breath, water) and then sit or stand quietly and listen for what teachings and perspectives arise. When you have received the guidance, bow and offer gratitude again and see if they need anything in return from you.

I like to think these practices diminish disconnectedness from the natural world and help us see our place and responsibility to the environment that nourishes and holds us.

Starr Potts, MA, MSW, LICSW
dreamweaversrwe@gmail.com
www.StarrPotts.com

Nature as Resource: Clarification Constellation

The beauty of constellation work is that there is the potential to support the introduction of an individual to a variety of fields within nature. With constellation work one is able to clarify which aspects within nature are actually a resource for a particular individual.

There are a number of the constellation templates that can serve to distill for one who feels under-resourced, where in Nature might they most easily encounter regeneration. Is it with the trees, is it with the sky, is it with a particular animal, or perhaps a bird, the wind, or the sea?

What is most powerful about this constellation experience is that it can facilitate an individual being able to identify a specific resource in a concrete way. If one sees through a constellation that there is indeed a deep resonance with the grass and one's self, it is a platform to develop meditations which are viscerally constructive.

This may also help to pinpoint at which juncture do my soul and nature meet most easily?

To begin a Nature as Resource Constellation the facilitator can interview the client to begin to consider what are the elements in nature that the person considers restorative. Which practices, or which elements does the seeker enjoy.

After an exchange with the client, representatives may be placed. Multiple nature beings should be placed by the client, and included will be a representative of the client. As the constellation unfolds, there may be surprises as well as confirmations. In the movement, and felt-sense of the representatives one is able to witness where there is resonance, or synergy. It may be that something that one thought was a resource, is not as reinforcing as one believed. An example, or instance, might be when one has perceived the beach as a resource, if the client's representative is uncomfortable, and has somatic discomfort, too much heat and even itching on the skin, what may be revealed is that the client experiences extreme sunburn when going to the beach. It can become clear that what was considered a form of stress-reduction and rejuvenation, accumulatively has been an uncomfortable experience. This can provide insight, allowing one to review, without judgment, which elements in nature actually provide nourishment.

And, it may also be that there is a surprising depth of relationship between the sunrise and the client. The specifics for each person are unique. Reinforcing that there is nothing to criticize, and inviting the client to witness the exchange between different experiences in nature and varied natural environments can help a person to clarify what really does support them.

Nature Constellation Exercise: Are you my teacher?

This is a constellation which encourages the facilitator's ability to embody the field, particularly in the exploration of a relational experience with nature.

Instructions are given:

Each individual in the group is going to be invited to take a walk outside. In quiet, stay open with the question, in facing the elements of nature:

Are you my teacher?

One may have exchange with trees, grass, insects, rocks, birds. Simply very slowly exploring the different elements in nature, waiting until there is the kind of recognition that one feels in a constellation when there is a connection.

Although there will be other participants outside as well, please do not engage each other in conversation as that is a distraction and the primary focus is to solicit which element of nature in this location is willing to commit to sharing with you as your teacher.

We will take 15 minutes outside. Please come in as soon as the time is up as a courtesy to the others who need your participation in this exercise to be able to access a deeper learning.

When you are finished, and you have 'felt' who your teacher is, thank your teacher and return to your seat. Do not disturb nature- do not take anything from the land, return to your seat with an awareness of the recognition of your 'teacher' and their energy field. Please hold the space in respect and as we wait for everyone to return and quietly spend the time listening and feeling into what your experience is in relation to your new found teacher.

When everyone arrives, you will find a partner. In dyads you will take turns representing the 'teacher' of your partner, and subsequently yourself. Each will have 5 minutes to face their teacher. You will first follow any movement, just tracking the felt sense of your representation while being careful of your own body and respecting the safety of the other. One will represent the teacher- the other will have opportunity to 'see' the eyes of their teacher. At 4 minutes, you will have opportunity to say one sentence to your teacher. The teacher will have opportunity to say one sentence to the student.

After the teacher has spoken, the student finds a movement in the body which expresses appreciation- or simply says a sincere thank you.

After this constellation, the two in the dyad will switch places, so that each has opportunity to face their teacher. Again, spend 4 minutes in exploring movement, the field of the teacher, and in the remaining minute you will have opportunity to exchange one sentence. The student may ask a question, or make a statement- one sentence.

This offers an opportunity to confront the western mind which has a tendency to want to pontificate. The precision and clarity of one sentence encourages the deep contact with the field and humble listening for what the teacher actually would like to say- not just what I think the 'student' wants or needs to hear.

Note: There are some individuals who have found the agreement of the 'teacher' was long term and their awareness of that element in nature, and the way in which they feel resourced by it became a part of their life.

Seeds:

Growing up on the tropical, equatorial island of Singapore, my friends and I mostly stayed out of the sun. As children we played in the garden when the sun went down, went swimming in the evenings, and went running early in the mornings or late in the day. With a focus on the mind and the intellect, I spent less time in nature and more indoor. Except for when we went to the beach. I have always loved being near the ocean. It's where I feel most at home.

My first nature constellation weekend began painfully. It was an unbearably hot, humid July morning. I was melting, uncomfortable and miserable. My sunscreen ran into my eyes and it stung. Later that weekend, we went out to look at nature and see if nature had a message. There was a group of day lilies and as I looked at them, gently waving in the slight breeze they said, "We see you." The message was comforting and spoke to the challenge I was facing at the time of being unseen.

Fast-forward a year later, on a crisp, fall day with a chill in the air. My t'ai chi class was practicing outdoors in a park. Our group leader spoke to me of a large oak tree. She said she spoke to the tree and the tree replied. "Hold your hands out," she instructed me, "and send warmth to the tree. It will send you heat." I did as she suggested, holding my palms out towards the tree, and like magic, the tree sent me a blast of heat. The heat felt so good that morning. I felt my whole body relax as I received the unexpected gift from nature delivered by the tree.

Another year later, and my mom and I were in our ancestral village, outside Jaffna, Sri Lanka. For the first time, I saw so many people who looked like me. And standing on the red sandy ground, I sensed and felt the energy of my ancestors. I felt it in specific areas that were impacted by the 30-year-old civil war, I felt the horror there. I felt it in our home, which had been requisitioned by the military during the war. The energy was palpable. I felt that connection to the land of my ancestors, my land, and my people.

Since then, I've begun paying more attention to nature when I go out. I look forward to exploring more than just the seas and the oceans when I speak with nature. Who knows what other magical gifts are in store for me? I look forward to finding out.

– Popsy Kanagaratnam, Constellations Facilitator & Coach
popsy.kanagaratnam@gmail.com

Forest Baths for our Brain: The Neuroscience of Nature Constellations

By Sarah Peyton

Before we knew as much as we know now about the way that the climate crisis is impacting the subarctic, melting the permafrost and threatening the boreal forest, I took part in a nature constellation with Francesca Mason Boring for the first time. She invited us each to be called into the constellation as a part of the ecosystem of the Eastern side of the Cascade Mountains in the Pacific Northwest of the United States. I waited for intuition to come, to move me into the constellation as some element of that part of nature, a process that is called "representing." I waited and waited, and I worried.

In Nature Constellations, people are called in to represent different elements of ecosystems. As they enter, they state who they are, and find the best place for themselves in the space where the constellation is being held. Some people are called in as trees, feeling the leaves or the pine needles as a part of their bodies. Some people are called in as the wind, and move fluidly through the constellation. Some come in as soil, some as insects or pollinators, some as flower species, some as large or small mammals. Within the constellation, the representatives often form close relationships with other elements of the constellation.

I was being called into this particular constellation as a tree, a very specific type of tree, one that was not a part of this ecosystem. So, I didn't enter, I just stayed on the sidelines and worried. I wasn't being called in to the constellation as an element of the Eastern Cascades ecosystem at all – I was being called in as a black spruce from the ecosystem of Interior Alaska, where I was born. Even though I hadn't entered the constellation, I felt this tree in my body. I felt the thin scales of bark as my own skin, and smelled the spruce sap in the air around me.

Black spruce trees are narrow, twisty, and spiky, with branches that droop and then turn up at the tips. Where I grew up they were a dusty black-green that covered the hills north of my home. The closer the black spruce are to the tundra, the shorter and spikier the trees become, adapting to the harsher conditions of the higher altitudes and the more northern latitudes. My favorite dreams are when I dream that I'm barefooted in the snow among the black spruce with the moon shining down on me.

The spruce form shapes in the snow that look like the pen and ink drawings that Santiago Ramón y Cajal made of the neurons of the brain. I am a lover of neuroscience. I think about the brain when I think about trees, since trees are so often shaped like neurons. The bark of the black spruce also reminds me of neurons. It starts out a reddish brown, and then as the spruce gets older, the bark becomes darker, with large, irregularly shaped, thin scales that look like the middle layers of the cerebral cortex in the human brain. In the fractals of nature, trees speak to me of nature's intelligence and the vast networks of communication that make up ecosystems.

And by bringing up brains in this context, is there a reduction of nature constellations to pieces, and are they stripped of meaning? Whenever we start to talk about the brain, especially in the context of something as beautiful and inclusive as Nature Constellations, we might begin to worry that we will be pulled out of the beauty and the spirituality into something banal, that strips the life from this inviting ritual form. But the beauty of the brain is that, when we look at it through the lens of the systemic, it is itself another form of nature constellations.

This lets us wonder, what is happening in the constellation of the brain when it participates in Nature Constellations?

Research shows us that any exposure to or immersion in nature is hugely supportive of human well-being. Over 100 studies have shown that being in nature, living near nature, or even viewing nature in paintings and videos can have positive impacts on our brains, bodies, feelings, thought processes, and social interactions.[1] So what the brain is constellating in Nature Constellations is healing and integration.

A particular kind of Nature Therapy, Shinrin-Yoku (Forest Bathing), which invites a mindful immersion into nature using all five senses, has been a subject of research, showing benefits to:

(1) the immune system function (increase in natural killer cells/cancer prevention);

(2) cardiovascular system (hypertension/coronary artery disease);

(3) the respiratory system (allergies and respiratory disease);

(4) depression and anxiety (mood disorders and stress);

(5) mental relaxation (Attention Deficit/Hyperactivity Disorder) and;
(6) human feelings of "awe" (increase in gratitude and selflessness)[2]

Current scientific findings are illuminating what humans intuitively know: nature has great benefits for the human brain and this is shown through increased happiness, health/well-being and cognition.[3] Nature Therapy offers the perspective that the ability to connect, integrate and feel complete with nature are important "happiness factors"; their loss can damage overall well-being and cause psychiatric and health difficulties, including making people more vulnerable to trauma. Nature Therapy emphasizes the importance of the creative process and non-verbal ways of working in helping the individual strengthen connections with the imagination, the emotions and the body.[4]

In order to heal from trauma and be trauma resilient, we need psychological, spiritual and community resources. Nature constellations are in part a form of Nature Therapy, and in part a form of direct connection with the planet, something altogether apart from and even more sacred than therapy, and they provide all three types of resources, linking us with the earth and its ecosystems, with a sense of something that is beyond the human, and with one another in the experience of representing.

We desperately need nature, and awe. We need reenchantment. In 2007, Charles Taylor's book, *A Secular Age*, was published. In this book, Taylor used the word *disenchantment* to describe the long process that started in the 16th century, whereby we came to believe that "the only locus of thoughts, feelings, spiritual élan is what we call minds" and that "the only minds in the cosmos are those of humans." This process depended on the "buffering" of the self, the separation of human minds from the bodies and material orders that our bodies are supposed to be connected to. In the world of "buffered selves" as he describes it, the material cosmos is drained of meaning and animate vitality, available to be managed by the forces of instrumental reason and technological control.[5]

The reenchantment process is described by neuroscience synthesist and philosopher Iain McGilchrist, in his book The Matter with Things: "What is required (in perceiving the world) is an attentive response to something real and other than ourselves, of which we have only inklings at first, but which comes more and more into being through our response to it – if we are truly responsive to it."[6] This process of being in relationship is what is most clearly invited by participation in nature constellations.

According to McGilchrist, the human brain has two ways of perceiving the world: one as mechanical, in pieces, a world which is put together and ruled by the human brain, located largely in the left hemisphere, and another way of perceiving -- one that can begin to apprehend the world as an irreducible whole, an intricate and finely-working, interdependent, multi-level system from which nothing can be removed or is disposable. This point of view is dependent on access to the right hemisphere. If this is true, nature constellations awaken and make accessible our right hemispheres. They do this in a number of ways:

- When we are brought into a depth of interconnection with other elements, we get to transcend human mistrust and have relationships with other human bodies, perhaps for the first time in our lives, awakening us to the possibility of non-traumatic relationships and bonding with other human beings;

- By moving us into profound relationality and a lived sense of interdependence with other elements of the Nature Constellation, thus nourishing a lived sense of ourselves as part of this planet's ecosystems;
- By awakening us to the big-picture of ecosystems and the planet;
- And more.

Moving to the systemic, big-picture lens (into the right hemisphere) -- whether we are looking at brains, at constellations, or at the ecosystems of the world and humans as a part of them – is a wonderful remedy for disconnection. Research reveals that exclusion and alienation hurt humans – that they register in the pain network of the brain,[7] creating an un-homed sense of hurt. The movement toward inclusion restores people, their stress systems and their immune systems. Nature constellations invite people into connection with one another and into a sense of home with this beloved planet we live on, which makes this type of constellation work a remarkable resource for us all. The more home we feel on the earth, the more care we take with the land.

Coming back to the Eastern Cascades, there I was, being called into the Nature Constellation as an element that was not part of that ecosystem. The dilemma of being called into a constellation as an element outside of the community being officially explored is a theme for me, both inside and outside of constellations. I teetered on the edge of participation, feeling the spruce inside me, and simultaneously respecting the facilitator's specific invitation. I am often in relationship with myself as an outsider. It is a familiar problem for me, but one in which the person holding the space, or setting the frame, is rarely as inclusive and welcoming as this facilitator was. And because we are talking about a profoundly relational form of sacred practice, her welcome mattered to me. It allowed me to enter as the element I was called to be, with all its foreignness and all its not belonging, and in the process, my lens on what this Nature Constellation was holding was widened. These things are all happening on the level of the constellation inside the brain, as well as on the level of the constellation in the room. The right hemisphere sees the big picture, and mine was working to hold a global ecosystem, in which the black spruce is important to the Eastern Cascades, and to Patagonia, and to the Sahara Desert.

With a personal welcome, even though I was worried about doing the constellation "wrong," I stood up to enter anyway, and a deep feeling of rightness and connection to the earth I first knew intimately flooded into me. As a result of my participation in that particular nature constellation, I am still partly the black spruce. Without the facilitators invitation to come into the constellation, I would not have the connection I have with the ecosystem I was born into, and a lived sense of that ecosystem as part of the world's whole. This nourishes a sense of connection and constellational belonging that keeps making deeper and deeper sense as we step more fully into an understanding of the global interrelationship of the destruction that is coming from rising temperatures and the climate crisis on our planet.

[1]*https://greatergood.berkeley.edu/article/item/what_happens_when_we_reconnect_with_nature*, harvested June 1, 2022.

[2]Shinrin-Yoku (Forest Bathing) and Nature Therapy: A State-of-the-Art Review, Margaret M. Hansen, Reo Jones, Kirsten Tocchini. Int J Environ Res Public Health. 2017 Aug; 14(8): 851. Published online 2017 Jul 28. doi: 10.3390/ijerph14080851

PMCID: PMC5580555

[3]Ibid.

[4] Berger, Ronen, and Maya Tiry. "The Enchanting Forest and the Healing Sand—Nature Therapy with People Coping with Psychiatric Difficulties." The Arts in Psychotherapy 39.5 (2012): 412–416. Web.

[5]*https://lareviewofbooks.org/article/the-trouble-with-re-enchantment/* harvested Feb. 10, 2022.

[6]McGilchrist, Iain. The Matter with Things. Perspectiva Press: 2021.

[7] Bernstein MJ, Claypool HM. Social exclusion and pain sensitivity: why exclusion sometimes hurts and sometimes numbs. Pers Soc Psychol Bull. 2012 Feb;38(2):185-96. doi: 10.1177/0146167211422449. Epub 2011 Sep 1. PMID: 21885860.

Bio: Sarah Peyton is a neuroscience education, constellations facilitator, certified Nonviolent Communication trainer and internationally published author who invites audiences into a compassionate understanding of the effects of relational trauma on the brain, and teaches about how to use resonance to change and heal.

Group Exercise: Forest Bathing/Shirin Yoku Constellation

The term Shirin Yoku was introduced in 1982 by the Japanese Ministry of Agriculture, Forestry and Fisheries. As with many modern reintroductions of the benefit of being in communion with nature, this practice of walking though the forest in a contemplative state was actually influenced by ancient Shinto and Buddhist practice which encourage allowing nature to be experienced through seeing, hearing, touching, smelling and tasting.

In addition to the experience of connection to nature, for those who are plagued by feelings of isolation, or for those who perceive human connection as a threat, or fictitious, this is a gentle experiential introduction to interrelatedness.

The experience of walking in a quaking aspen forest is transcendent. The bark of the tree is white with bits of starkly contracting dark patches. The leaves are green and reflect the light, making a spring or summer forest iridescent. In the fall the leaves are a golden yellow, and in the summer there is a quiet stand of sentries, all white, often surrounded by snow. According to the National Forest Foundation, the oldest know 'clone' (the name for the large stand of Aspen, as they are genetically identical -all coming from the same roots) is in Utah, USA at the Fishlake National Forest and is reported to be 80,000 years old.

It is possible in a group to place multiple representatives for the trees in the quaking aspen forest, and rotate the invitation for others who are in the group to walk through the forest as human beings. Simply with an openness to taking in the benevolence, the energy, the conversation of the trees, representatives of both the human beings and the trees may embody a sense of deep connection. In this constellation not only are participants able to experience a form of tree bathing, they are able to experience the field of connection of one of the earth's largest organisms.

In this format it is important to encourage participants to separate their own sense of drama or trauma regarding the state of nature in a general sense, from what is genuinely being represented by the trees in the constellation.

This template is simple. To prepare for the constellation cut strips of paper from a standard copy size of paper. Cut pieces of paper so that they are 2" wide X 8" long. You will have at least five strips of paper from each business size sheet of paper. Cut enough strips of paper to exceed the number of participants by several (in the event papers stick together during the constellation- the process will not be interrupted).

The number of representatives of human beings depends upon the size of the group. If you have a group of fifteen, you may have three participants who initially represent human beings walking through the aspen forest. If you have a group of twenty, you may choose to begin with four participants who represent human beings. The majority of the participants will be representatives of trees in a forest. A lesser number of representatives will be representing themselves- as human beings, and will take some time walking through the forest.

In a group of eight participants, or more, invite the representatives of the aspen forest to stand and gradually find their place in the space. If the constellation is outdoors, for the sake of acoustics, encourage the group to stay within an accessible distance.

In this constellation it is important to invite representatives of the trees to stand as members of a quaking aspen colony. Invite the trees of the forest to the representational perception of being a tree within this community of trees, which are sometimes identified as a single living organism. Some representatives of the trees in the forest may even become aware of the expanse of the process of respiration and photosynthesis. Quaking aspens grow together, sharing roots, multiplying by sending up new roots which become the new baby trees, unlike many species of trees which have 'seedlings' which come from seeds of the parent trees.

Depending upon your group size and character, you may either make a space for each participant to experience the tree bathing constellation, or you may have a limited number of participants walk through, and then call together a talking circle to allow both trees and tree bathers to share their experience.

Integration: Debriefing is optional, and depending upon the nature of your group there are several options if there is a sense that it is helpful.

- It is possible to support integration by having everyone in the group come together after the Forest Bathing Constellation. If the group is grounded in mindfulness, it may be that the most supportive approach is to have everyone sit in silence together as they individually and collectively integrate their experience.

- It is possible to introduce a group meditation to support integration of this constellation experience. It may be a guided meditation which allows the embodied experience to be expanded to a visualization that is portable, something that participants can duplicate when they have left the workshop.
- The facilitator may also encourage break out groups, or dyads to give participants the opportunity to share a bit about their experience and poignant insights.

With the forest bathing constellation what is reinforced is that the field of trees can be transported in an instant into an indoor space, or even confinement. It may be that the benefits of the aroma of the trees are not an immediate presence, but in fact, for some, the memory of the sound of the trees is what returns to them, as they make their way through the 'forest' of representatives.

It may also occur that participants begin to distinguish between the monkey mind of human people and the literally 'rooted' countenance of tree people.

Me and my Tree- Constellation/Exercise- Dyad

This constellation has been quite powerful for some participants. There are two representatives:

Me (self-represented)

My Tree

Participants are invited before the dyads are selected to sit quietly and think for a moment about a favorite tree. It may be a tree from childhood, it may be a tree that they pass on the way to work, or it may be a tree in their yard.

The facilitator invites them to take their time and think of the smell, the seasons, the experience of the seeing, being with, or perhaps climbing the tree.

Before breaking into dyads, participants are reminded to simply feel into their bodies and notice what is there. Encourage participants not to talk or have verbal exchange for the first few moments, just to look at their tree, while the representative for the tree tracks their sense of relationship to their partner, and begins to breathe into anything they notice about being a representative for a tree.

The group is then broken into pairs. First one representative stands for the tree of the other and the partner is able to face the representative of their tree.

Tell the group that you will signal (with a bell- or simply directions) when it is time for verbal exchange. Remind the participants that they do not want to hinder the voice of the tree by inventing their own narrative. This exchange is to articulate what is coming from the field, what is genuine, what is more likely in keeping with the quiet of a tree conversation. Invite participants to hold the structure of the exchange:

The person witnessing their tree may have a question or a statement;

The tree may respond.

When the exercise is complete the pair will switch representations so each participant is able to experience 'their' tree, and each of the persons in the dyad is also able to experience representing the tree.

After several minutes close the exercise and invite a short round, either inviting everyone to make a statement about their experience, or invite spontaneous sharing, assuring that anyone who wants to have their experience undisturbed is encouraged not to speak, but to simply be open to the sharing of others.

This constellation description is deceptively simple. In more than one instance the exchange between a human and their tree has been very deep. On one occasion the representative for the tree stated clearly, "I am not the tree that you imagined- I am the tree that was there for you when you were a child." The representative for the tree then went on to describe a very specific event and a very specific way in which the client would interact with the tree. The tree wanted to remind that not only had it been available throughout the difficulty, but that in fact they had a relationship.

The client and the representative for the tree did not know each other prior to the tree constellation, so the specificity and accuracy were startling. But the memory was also informing. There had already been a very real experience of communicating with a tree, and as an adult the client was able to fully honor and thank the tree that had been there at such a difficult juncture.

The Nature of Time in Nature Constellations

Family Systems Constellation, and subsequently Nature Constellations have had to make friends with the conversation regarding time.

Routinely, systems are examined in a way which includes, past, present and future. We often find the schism or trauma in the past which created a pattern which impedes progress or wellbeing in the present and when we have identified, acknowledged, and addressed the barriers which were invisible but pervasive- there is the possibility for the emergence of brighter, more informed, future.

In constellations we encounter linear, cyclical and vertical time. Linear time is our clocked time which has a beginning and end. Cyclical time includes the organic flow of the seasons, while vertical time is the time experienced in mindfulness, without boundary or judgment, simply being in the space between heaven and earth.

There are numerous descriptions regarding the philosophical understanding and perception of time. Suffice it to say that there is not just one aspect of time which is present in constellations. There are times when the clock seems to stop, times when our perception is that a series of generational traumas are viewed in an instant. The best a facilitator can do is to normalize whichever aspect of time is present and to help participants assimilate the perceived flux which can be unusual for a western linear audience.

Some cultures speak of 'dream time'. This is a perspective which must be given a place when it is integral to the system. The importance of time and timeliness may vary from culture to culture: rubber time, Indian time, are some cultural definitions which indicate that time is flexible, not fixed.

Many cultures embrace the concept of reincarnation, a cyclical rebirth which has various implications for our conscious walk in this lifetime.

Our modern, linear perception of our importance in time on this planet contributes to levels of anxiety regarding the environment, which can impede our ability to act. Constellation are one tool which can support our finding our place in the grand scheme, in an appropriate way. The earth came first, and so did most things in creation. Everything in its time.

Seeds:

Nature tracks for us the passage of memory, is its own storyteller, and the energies of all possibility. If not about past lives, the flurry of leaves and wind to signal a wise message, the unmistakable animal appearance or sound that leaves us stopped in OUR tracks -- nature speaks, dances, and breathes through us and to us.

Candice Wu, SEP, MA, CYT 500
https://candicewu.com

Constellation Group Exercise: Time line walking mediation

This is a time in which some experience extreme anxiety regarding the state of the planet. When individual fears of apocalyptic destruction of the earth, pollution, or climate change are overwhelming it is difficult to serve as a 'hollow bone' when looking at issues regarding nature.

Looking at aspects of nature utilizing systems constellation requires some level of grounded openness. To be prepared to acknowledge a new perspective or insight, having the capacity to separate from hysteria is a pre-requisite. Acute eco-anxiety, ecological grief, severe eco-trauma, all are descriptions of a level of emotional distress regarding climate change and our human impact upon the environment which may make it difficult for one to commit to a neutral, open, and non-judgmental stance. These are essential for representative perception to emerge in an unhindered way.

Fortunately, there is a very embodied way in which students, workshop participants and human beings in general can began to experience our place in the timeline of the planet.

In order to support the possibility of humility and context, this group exercise, which I like to present as a walking meditation, is a wonderful way for participants in nature constellations to ground in the antiquity of the planet.

What is required is a single roll of toilet paper, volunteers who are comfortable with numbers assure the process is accurate. As the roll of toilet paper is completely rolled out, it is good to have some space.

There are placards that are placed at particular counts on the line of rolled out toilet paper that indicate epochs of time in the earth's history.

I recommend cutting each of the epochs of time out and laminating them. This gives them more structural integrity when you place them along the line of toilet paper and gives you opportunity to reuse the same epoch labels.

This exercise is an embodied introduction to context, experiencing a felt sense of our place in the system and time.

Kronos, (sequential time and calendars) is one perception of time. Kairos is an expanded experience of time, spiritual time, and includes an unknown and even seductive future.

In the past this "constellation" or walking meditation, has taken place with the roll or toilet paper rolled out indoors, at times utilizing the length of a building, hallways, main meeting room, and offices. In one instance, two facilitators: Rotger Heilmeier and Lin Geng, actually placed the toilet paper in a circular fashion, creating a wonderful walking labyrinth. This spiral layout is something I intend to use again in the future. It provides opportunity to have the full length of the toilet paper within one room, while still allowing space for a number of participants to quietly walk the 'labyrinth' allowing space in between each person. The full length of the toilet paper roll delineates the various epochs

This activity has also taken place outdoors- preferably when there is no wind. These are two website references for this exercise, but you can find several descriptions and directions by asking 'Auntie' Google to show you 'toilet paper and epochs of time'.

What is important for participants to understand is that the toilet paper labyrinth represents only 65 million years in the 4.6 billion geological clock, of the Earth. This journey only engages consideration of the Paleocene epoch (55-65 million years ago), to the Holocene epoch, which includes 10,000 years ago to present. As one walks the length of the roll, passing designated geological time periods, it is a revelation to find that human beings only appear on the last fraction of the last square of the toilet paper roll.

https://www.sciencelearn.org.nz/resources/483-toilet-roll-geologic-timescale

https://www.earthlearningidea.com/PDF/234_Toilet_roll_of_time.pdf

Seeds:

I had planned to make a last little constellation exercise in small groups but a question "How many generations do you set up?" brought me to something else.

Constellation: Everybody had a role, first client, parents, grandparents, then one representative for great grandparents; and we went on: 100 generations back, 1000, early human being, link between animal and human being, animal, plant, bacteria - everybody could choose the own role - (there are so many possible!)- finally, "life" standing on a chair.

At the beginning they all looked to the client. Then the client turned also looking into the future to the following generations. Then he turned, and slowly everybody else turned, step by step, feeling what is behind and looking what he is coming from. So then everybody looked to life. Then they made together a deep bow. And then spontaneously I let life also turn and bow. -Bertold Ulsamer, Facilitator, Germany

Elk Teachings for Family & Human Systems Constellation

It's finally springtime. Winter was quiet, the snow was deep, the nights were cold, accumulatively weeks with below zero weather, which allows for a persistent walk with humility. No one is greater than freezing temperatures. Some of our local bear and trees, and most of the plants, retreat, bowing fully to the reality of the freeze. In fact, this helps me with my facilitation of family constellations and perhaps my approach to living systems. Not every creature responds the same to frigid cold, or the heat for that matter. To be forgiving and recognize the body response to various elements within family and systems constellation can be crucial. I have no impulse to judge the bear for sleeping, or the ermine for loving the snow. It is just as important, for safety's sake to be cognizant of what is realistic and comfortable for every being when we are walking in the field of Family Constellations.

Life is emerging everywhere. I cannot help but be encouraged. When I look out the window and see the elk, I am happy to count the yearlings. Before I know it some of the elk will clearly develop as bull elks with their imposing antlers. Shortly after that emergence I will be watching to see who is pregnant, and then will come the best part of the year, I will face my uncontrollable laughter as I watch the new calves compete, still try to find their footing and when they need to be replenished, they will find their mothers. Rhythm and biology are present in life; when I facilitate, I honor that. Here, surrounded by the natural world, I am aware that there are some cows who will not have calves; some of their calves may die. Sometimes cows are barren and some of them, as one elder pointed out to me, even grow antlers. To know that nature and life determine destiny in a way that is beyond critique does not need my interpretation. It just is. This allows me to breathe in deeply all the oxygen that the trees and grasses and buck brush so generously gift me. And, when I am facilitating constellations, this breathing in allows me to have a heart that is fully open to what life decided in the history of some family systems.

In the Spring, when I begin to plant, I am reminded that there are many places where we have choice and agency. We have opportunities to decipher what is innate and what is an option. In my gardening I practice xeriscape, which means that I plant native plants as much as possible and do not impose my expectations upon those who are not adapted to this place and way of living. For fruit trees there is rainwater that has been collected from the runoff of the roof. I am reminded when I travel that these plants do not need me. They exhibit the strength of those who are in the right place. They are at home. I may visit when I can but their life and subsistence are bigger than me. They are my teachers, not dependent upon my intrusion and they flourish beyond what I could engender. They teach me about awe, and they remind me that when we are in our right place, we are healthy, resilient, and productive. I am reminded that this is really what most are looking for when they come for a constellation, just a simple reminder about the belonging and strength that is a yearning and foundation of our nature.

In so many ways the natural world supports the stance of the facilitator. To have the widest view, to be unafraid of the beauty, to have a place for the loss and the changes, to fully inhale and exhale, and know that the life-giving breath does come from somewhere and it freely nurtures us. Watching the elk reminds me to have my feet fully on the ground. When I watch the elk, I am reminded to eat when I'm hungry, rest when I'm tired, and try to stay in my body in a fluid and effortless way.

My awareness, in the moment is gratitude that when I am blessed to sit in a Constellation Circle, the elk come with me.

All My Relations

Elk Teaching: The Treasure of Invisibility and The Invitation to Be Seen

4am. I'm sound asleep when I am roused by the startling sound of a bull elk bugling just outside my bedroom window. It's pitch- black outside, a startling wake-up call and truly out of the ordinary to have the elk so close to the house. Being in a rural area in North Eastern Washington State, we have seen an increase in elk traffic since so many fires have engulfed surrounding habitat over the past several years; it is not a rarity to see these beautiful neighbors in the daytime, but it was rare to hear a bull-elk bugle right outside the window- in the dark of night. A fully grown bull elk can weigh 700-1100 pounds, and is easily 5'tall at the shoulders, definitely plenty of room for a healthy set of lungs! I didn't want to turn on the porch light. We sleep with no lighting inside or out with all the windows open. Our wildlife neighbors can have the evenings to themselves and we have the benefit of country air accompanying our sleep.

Elk, particularly in the fall, when the bulls are in rut, travel in large family groups. Thirty elk is not unusual to see, one neighbor on a side road by the river saw a herd of 60 and in some areas, herds can be as large as 200-400.

After 10 minutes or so, as I was debating going back to sleep, I heard another elk call, this time on the other side of the house.

My husband woke, and we both quietly walked the circumference of the inside of the house to experience the excited chatting of a substantial gathering. We could not see them, but within minutes, the whole of the house was surrounded by elk, deep in conversation, chirping, whistling, growling, the volume and intensity of the conversation, in surround sound is impossible to describe. Bulls, cows, and elk calves each contributed something to the lively convention.

We were invisible, the house was invisible. Not making a sound, not interfering, the magic of not being seen, allowed the experience of being directly in the middle of a very vocal assembly. They wandered around the yard eating pears, elderberries, chomping on buck brush on the hill side.

This community conversation continued for fully two hours, until the sun began to rise, and they gradually began to spread out over the ridge, still calling to each other and perhaps being joined by others, judging by the development of the symphony.

An encounter like this is rare. From an indigenous perspective, when nature presents you with an occurrence that is well outside of the norm, it is a good time to listen for something deeper. It is time to be ready to absorb all the gifts that have come wrapped in that encounter. This is akin to being in what in constellation work we call the knowing field.

Still in awe, we made coffee and then I stepped outside to listen to what had become the emergence of dawn. A stillness, then the gradual introduction of bird celebrations. Autumn was coming, and with the light I was aware that new colors were beginning to emerge in the landscape.

Some of the color pallets in this area are stunning. Deep awareness began to come to my bones. The Elk hoedown would have stopped, if at any moment we had not been concealed by the night. If we had turned on the lights, or spoken loudly, they are still wild beings and when they feel disturbed, they walk away, or even run in the opposite direction. I was aware of the benefit that being out of sight had provided, and I was also aware that nature was coming into the season in which she does her level best to teach us about visibility. No fear of being too garish, autumn is when the land teaches us not just about the beauty of change, but the elegance of being seen.

Having had the privilege of being allowed to walk with many as they have looked at transgenerational barriers in their personal and professional life, I have become keenly aware of how often the challenge of visibility and feeling invisible can be a difficulty. Part of the burden of feeling unseen often has the adjunct of not feeling heard, not having a voice. From a systems constellation perspective we can be amazed that our hesitation to step forward, or say our piece can have its foundation in our being loyal to a systemic prohibition against being too loud, too flashy, or too boisterous. There can also be personal traumas that render one mute and wanting to hide, but if we are to look for a trusted mentor to support coming forward and shining in an organic way, one has only to look to nature.

There are a variety of good modalities which can encourage our rewiring in a way that allows us to no longer be frozen, but whether our timidness be concept driven, or the result of a systemic family block, the voice of the elk, and the exhibition of autumn foliage are worth breathing in.

Western culture has in recent history been driven by the head. The majority of the indigenous cultures and wisdom traditions honor clear thinking, but often give greater esteem to the heart. If we listen to the elk and see the brilliant landscape with our hearts, things become discernible that we may not otherwise have perceived.

There are times when not being seen or heard may have advantage. But there is a world of difference between *choosing* silence or invisibility and being frozen.

If you have the time, if you are able to look and listen to Nature, you can be sure that she will have something to say. My guess is that she will tell you that you are too beautiful not to be seen and your voice has a place in the world. Perhaps that is what the elk were speaking about.

As constellation work has developed, in this time of historical challenges, including the field of nature becomes an essential to fully support those who are looking for connection, and even courage. Sharing a few examples of the grounding that comes from such a resource may be helpful for facilitators who have not considered nature as an extension of our human systems. Perhaps considering some possibilities will further encourage those who intuitively felt a need to acknowledge that we, our families and ancestors are a part of the natural world, and this natural world has held us and provided for us for generations.

As the work becomes more accessible, the participation in constellations will continue to expand. With any luck, the participation in systems constellation will include an exponentially diverse representation of our world.

Nature in some way or another is accessible to everyone. The sky can be seen by nearly every human being. The presence of the ground is present for all people, regardless of background. Mother Nature is a resource, once introduced, which can easily accompany workshop participants long after their personal constellation is done.

When we facilitate family constellations, there are times when one's family system or individual history is so riddled with trauma that it is difficult to fully facilitate or process a constellation without the client going into a state of overwhelm. There are a number of techniques that can be supportive: pacing, somatic work, stillness, breathing techniques, story, embodiment, there are a plethora of modalities that we have seen can enhance the safety of the container as well fortify both facilitator and client. To unconsciously dismiss all the resourcing that may be available within the actual landscape may be a dis-service to those who are looking for not only the hidden dynamics which create disorder, but also the hidden dynamics which may strengthen both themselves and their system.

Regarding the issue of painful invisibility, or fear of having a voice, there are common dynamics in the family system that can be explored:

- Did someone have to hide, or keep quiet to avoid abuse, capture or death during war?
- In the family system was there was rage, substance abuse, or systemic conditioning that licensed violence- and had to be avoided?
- Was there some inequity which prevented members of the family system from being able to assert themselves: slavery, economic disparity, having a different racial or ethnic background which systemically constricted one's confidence or recognition?
- Did someone hang for speaking out, or was there political oppression which restricted the voice in which too much visibility could be a death sentence?
- Was there a secret that had to be kept- sometimes including many within the family, or was the revelation of a secret something that came at great cost to a generation, or more, in a family system?

It may be that if these systemic deterrents to being seen or heard have been revealed and honored, the system can relax, but there may be times when even identification of the specific entanglements in the family system leave the seeker with a feeling of something not being complete.

When facilitating a constellation around the pain of not being able to speak or be seen, and there is a felt sense that the field of the constellation seems to be reaching for something further, it is realistic, and in some cases necessary to bring in the natural world of which we are all a part.

Resourcing one who is aching for permission to come out of hiding, when there is a yearning to speak in a self-assertive way which is not exaggerated or forced may require a facilitator to inquire and invite those aspects of nature which display a level of luminosity which is fully organic.

In a group it is possible to approach the inclusion of a support coming from the natural world in one of three ways.

- The client may be solicited for suggestions, "When you think of the natural world, where do you recognize some being which has ease with visibility?"
- The facilitator may take a cue from some element of nature which has been making itself entirely visible during the day: are there autumn trees that have been being blown by the wind, have there been bright yellow and black goldfinches resting on the foliage outside the window with persistence, do you notice peony blossoms on the blouses and shirts of a dozen participants, and an unlikely print on the wall which is presenting the same flower?
- Are participants able to center and in quiet feel into their body and natural beings who want to offer their innate wisdom regarding what is needed in the way of strengthening? Is it possible to solicit from the group, "First, being sure you have permission, is there some

element in nature that wants you to represent it, which offers support for this client? Placing a representative for "The client who is ready to be seen (or heard), invite a movement of the soul to encourage nature to fortify the representative, and by association the client as well.

When we allow nature to have a voice, or be seen around issues of needing to be concealed, we may be inviting the 'bigger hands' that have had such a part in the success of constellation work in general.

I invite you to expand your own experience about what Nature can teach about voice and visibility.

For just a moment, spend some time with each of the following, with open heart:

- A rainbow
- Thunder
- An azure pond
- Squawking geese
- Brilliant Sunset
- An elephant

Thousands have experienced unique relief for a host of difficulties through the seemingly simple movement of giving everyone withing the family a place. Being able to step into the world with greater wholeness and confidence has implications for well-being: body, mind and soul.

Adding a most obvious addition to support the family and the evolution of those who are on the hero's journey toward wellness is a necessity that is as 'clear as day'.

May we as facilitators see and hear all the support that is available to us in our walk as well.

All My Relations

Included with permission of The Knowing Field, Issue 37, January 2021

What is my rightful place in relation to the Land? Reflections and Observations from Land Constellations and the Knowing Field
by Tanja Meyburgh

Origins of this work: Start at your own back door

This work literally started at my own back door. Sue Davidoff and I have been developing this form of land constellations since 2016. We started with the land where we live, looking at the history of what happened. Both of us live in areas that were previously declared "whites only" areas during Apartheid. Before that it was farmed by the colonizers in Cape Town for the ships that came passing by. Much of the labour was done by enslaved people who were later set free and given land by these farmers in the area. Before all of that the land had been the hunting and gathering grounds and sacred sites of the indigenous San people of South Africa. So as we went through the layers and started to feel into what it meant to own this land and live there. We were aware of the pain and the suffering that was perpetrated on other people, in order for us to have that privilege.

We developed a workshop to acknowledge what had happened and bring awareness to people of the price that has been paid for ownership and the privilege of calling a place home. What we realized was that land is so deeply connected with our identity, it's so deeply connected with our belonging, and that if we look to the way that Indigenous people around the world have connected to land, it has been one of incredible mutual love and belonging, and bonding. Indigenous people belonged to the land as opposed to the land belonging to people.

We arrived at the question: "what will it take to come into right relationship with the land?". As human beings, we have exited a symbiotic relationship with land, and are taking more than the land has resource to give. We have lost our right relationship with the earth and the price is too high. So we acknowledge the history, acknowledge the people, acknowledge what happened. The healing movement shifts from ideas of *ownership* and *possession*, to *belonging, p*artnership, and a more symbiotic relationship with the land, rather than extracting and taking without limit. We are no longer in right relationship with the land. The land is ancient, it is older than all of us. It is big, and we are tiny and young in comparison.

I have seen what looks like an interrupted attachment to the mother - a similar movement happening in people who have been disconnected and dispossessed of their land. It's like a primal wound, like being ripped from the Mother, with the same consequence. Disconnection from the land and places of our belonging is a trauma.

It isn't just the land that was ripped away from people of colour, it's is their names, religions, connection with ancestry, culture, innocence, and purity. Another colleague working with me in land is Veronica King, who grew up as a black woman in Apartheid South Africa. The issue of land is a very deep part of who she is and how apartheid shaped her. Her parents never owned land, and the land that her grandparents owned was taken away from them. She says: "I've worked really hard. And I'm pleased to say that I own property now. Even that has been a struggle because the system of keeping black people disenfranchised, dispossessed colonized, in all ways, is still prevalent in South Africa and globally. We need to start recognizing, and acknowledging the impact that colonization all over the world has had on people that look like me. I've always just wanted to make White people comfortable, because I know, if they're not comfortable, I stand to lose a lot. Black people stand to lose a lot when we do not make White people comfortable."

Similarly to Veronica's experience, themes that have emerged in constellations centralising the land are colonization, dispossession, forced removals, immigration, refugees, different connection to different pieces of land, and even the fertility of the land being affected through what has been done and happened in those places.

What happens when we feel into what it is like to have a more Indigenous relationship with the land? One where the land is sacred, it's deep, it contains song lines and ancestors. It's a spiritual connection, a belonging to source and to all of creation. As modern people we have lost that connection. We don't greet the land or the ancestors of a place when we arrive somewhere new. We don't ask for permission or hold in reverence this ancient being that sustains us. We are disconnected, owning and abusing the land as a possession.

Further themes that have emerged in land work are: suppression of the feminine and women's access to land; ecological degradation, destruction and ecological grief; access to sacred sites and graves; war sites and unmarked graves; mining and extraction of resources; man-made borders;

And so how do we come into right relationship with the land? Where do we belong in the order of things? How do we stand in a position that allows the systemic healing for people, for nations, for territories, for individuals and for the collective?

What are we referring to as *land*?

In this work we have not clearly defined what we mean as land as so many people have different meanings they ascribe to this word, and in those different meanings lie their unique life experiences and consequent relationship to land. We found a division in why people relate to land systems that is broadly divided into:

- Ecological concern for land and environment
- Socio-political concern for the people

In multi-cultural groups, the ecological concern has been stronger in those who have had access to land and land ownership, those from colonising or first world countries, and privileged backgrounds. The socio-political concern for land, centres around land rights, the colonised and dispossessed and is held predominantly by those of different racial groups, countries that have been invaded or colonised, and political or gender activists.

Although the land is essentially all connected and experiences itself as one land, one earth. Through centralising the land many collective trauma themes have emerged in the groups, but always with this anchor of the land, and the anchor of the ancestors of the soil, those that lived and died on that land. We have been able to find resources in the grounding of working with the land that are common globally. Resources that restore connection.

Even though humans have split the land up into various borders and countries and properties, when we really go deeper into the soil and we start to look at what is the land actually expressing, the land is not affected by the borders. You can put down borders, but what lives in the land is borderless

The Compassionate Witness as transformative

This work requires a special kind of witnessing. Witnessing in a way that is really holding deep presence for the process. We invite participants in land constellations to work actively with the witnessing process: to focus during the constellation purely on each other, and on this process. Witnesses often feel a lot of discomfort, guilt, grief and somatic responses. There are all sorts of difficult feelings as we progress through the work. I invite participants to really see how it's possible to stay with the discomfort without trying avoid or get away from it or, but to really process it in their body. This is what we have the power to do. We can hold space for the voices that want to be heard in the constellation, and use our bodies to process the collective trauma. I'm aware that it may be deeply painful, or it may bring up guilt or shame. However, this is part of the work, and we welcome it, we don't want to exclude it. We consciously feel, let it be present in us, and we invite the ground beneath our feet that connects us to support us. It takes courage to look with compassion at things that make us uncomfortable, and to take our share to process these feelings through our bodies using the breath and the resources we have available to us. Land Constellations are collective work, for all of us that are here now, for all of our ancestors, for all of our descendants.

Important representations in Land Constellations 2018-2022

- Land
- Ancestors of the soil
- Water
- Indigenous / First people
- Animals and Plants
- Dispossessed people / Voiceless
- Masculine / Feminine / Gender relations
- Beneficiaries of Ill-gotten land gains
- Compensation
- Feminine / Masculine principles

Compensation

Essentially, wealthy modern societies are built on stolen land. Even though we can acknowledge what came before, and find ways to honour those that lived, died and we're buried in a place, we are seeing that it is not enough. We are not attempting to find solutions in this work as such, but rather to bring awareness, to begin a process of acknowledgment and seeing the voices, people and parts that have been excluded. As facilitators we remain humble to the enormity of this work and that we are only able to do small pieces, not to offer solutions. There is however a process of material compensation that appears needed in order for real systemic balance to come about. The consequence of ill-gotten gains continues to affect many generations beyond us. Acknowledgment is not enough to bring these systems into balance, but it is a starting point.

Individual and Collective Work

Its really important for Land Constellations to be effective, that there is a personal movement and a collective movement. Each of us is a fractal of the whole system, and simply doing a constellation without the internal movement does not bring healing. We sense into the field what needs to be seen, but we also look into ourselves at those parts that need to be acknowledged and integrated. As part of the collective we are able to process and digest systemic movements on a somatic level, one piece at a time. When we look at the colonizer or at the perpetrator in the constellation, the perpetrators are part of us, part of our ancestry too. They may have been displaced from their own ancestral lands or left their country of birth due to difficult circumstances or lack of opportunities. It is helpful to start at our own backdoor with the lands that we are closely related to, to process what lies in these relationships and in our somatic memory first before looking at wider systems.

We can then use the collective constellation in a specific way to look at the social, political, and what's underneath in the deer layers of the land. In these layers there are no borders, there are no nations, there are no countries. Participants can experience what it feels like to belong to the land and to feel connected to it. This is beyond laws created by humans, but rather the natural law of time hierarchy in relation to that which is so ancient. In honoring the stories of that land and everything that happened there, and the people that are buried in the soil, there is relaxation. These people - from both sides - are equal in death. They are no longer on opposite sides of the veil of life - they have become ancestors of that place, or as my teacher in Southern African lineage traditions calls them: t*he ancestors of the soil.* Here we have an opportunity to come into right relationship with the history, in the honoring of these ancestors. In honouring all of them, equal in death, honing their fate, acknowledging the history as it was and cannot be changed, we can come into a primary movement with the land. The land is relieved by this honoring, it brings peace to the land.

Stance of the Land Constellations Facilitator

Many of us in South Africa thought that with the with the fall of Apartheid and the subsequent Truth and Reconciliation Commission, we would have this beautiful rainbow nation and everything would just get better. There was so much hope and excitement and people wanted to do good and heal the nation, and I was one of them. A lot of attention was paid to the victims which was important, but very little attention was paid to the perpetrator. Many white people went into the guilt, the denial, and the avoidance of the perpetrator history and ancestry. The exclusion of this oppressor has led to continued perpetrations: what we reject we become, unconsciously. The tendency is to go out there and to want to fix and help and create lovely healing ceremonies for the victims, but very little acknowledgement of the privileges and ill-gotten gains that we still benefit from.

As a facilitator it is dangerous to step into the field to help while rejecting one's inner perpetrator. It's important to know why we do this work, and to tend to our own victim and perpetrator dynamic. It becomes dangerous when we want to do that work, because it's calling us, but we don't first do our own inner work. It may show up as microaggressions which are subtle or unintentional discriminations against members of marginalised groups. These are often related to the shadow parts of ourselves: "I'm not a racist," "All lives matter," "It wasn't me." These are the things that have a very deep, painful effect on people that are not in the dominant culture. Dominant voices exclude marginalised voices or the voiceless, and we need to take off our ancestral blindfolds and learn to see in new ways, not only the field, but ourselves and our client's position in history of the land.

Example mini-constellation for relationships with Place

People's relationship to land is different to the land itself, they relate to land primarily in four ways:

1. The land of their birth
2. The land where they now live
3. The land where their ancestors come from
4. Land that they feel spiritually connected to

In groups of two, set up the one of the above 1 to 4 without telling them who they represent, but knowing who they are. Set yourself up in relation to them. Allow movements to unfold - following the felt-sense in the body, without talking. Pay attention to your own internal landscape, the land that is represented, and the relationship between the two of you. Let the movement continue for 3 to 4 minutes. Close this mini-constellation, step out of your roles. Swop and let the other person set up land that they are connected to in the same way. At the end share your experiences for a few minutes, staying with what you felt in that role: feelings, sensations, observations rather than analysis or interpretation.

The intention of this exercise is to experience one's personal relationship to a particular place.

Ancestors of the Soil

Coming into contact with indigenous traditions and particularly the Southern African lineage tradition, I came to understand the importance of introducing oneself to the ancestors of the soil of a place, and the effect that they have on us when we live in a place. The Ancestors of the soil refer to all the people that have lived and died and been buried in a place. These ancestors are not necessarily of our own biological lineage, they could be both connected to our lineage or even those that perpetrated against our ancestors. In the soil, in death, there are all equal and do not hold the same conflicts and positions that they did once as human beings. In the tradition of native Americans and one of my teachers, Francesca Mason-Boring, I include all our relations in the honoring of the ancestors of the soil: the humans, the animals, the plants and the stones. All those tiny fragments of them contained in the soil when you look at it closely. They become part of us in the food that we eat from a place, and through the bare skin of the feet and the hands touching the soil. When we come to a new place we introduce ourselves, when we work with the earth, we seek permission from them. Being in good relation with these ancestors means that we are in our right place, as ones that have come later. We come with humility and respect for the past, and for those that were there first.

In all the constellations that we have facilitated about the land we have brought the ancestors of the soil in. In the same way as we might bring in the lineage ancestors for resource and support in a family constellation, or the founders in an organisation. The movement that heals and brings relief to the land is that acknowledgment and honouring of the ancestors of the soil, often spontaneously offered by a representative in the constellation in the form of a deep bow. We see that the healing movement comes when we come into right relationship to these beings.

Bio:

Tanja Meyburgh, counseling psychologist, founder of African Constellations, has taken 17 groups through a full two-year facilitation training and is the primary pioneer of constellations work in South Africa with 20 years of experience specializing in this field. More recently she co-founded Ancestral Connections integrating dance and constellations, the REAL Academy, an online resource for Embodied and Ancestral Learning, and completed a 20-day Systemic Constellation training for the Arabic World. Tanja has also presented at the international intensives in Germany, South Africa and Australasia, and accepted invitations to teach at conferences and workshops in Germany, Australia, Belgium, United Kingdom, Kuwait, Netherlands, Portugal, and the USA.

Tanja's MA (Psych) in Narrative Therapy has had a big impact on how she works with diverse cultures and views power relations and marginalized voices and communities. She also has training and experience in wilderness therapy, art therapy, expressive movement and South African lineage wisdom. Tanja provides a creative and experiential learning space that brings a sense of soul and spirit in a psychologically grounded way. Her interest in self-growth, personal and collective ritual and embodiment supports her to hold a broad and deep container for her clients' personal and professional process. Her work is described by those who know her as gentle and inclusive. Tanja lives in Cape Town, South Africa with her two children.

Seeds:

So, what I learned was really, that it is not just about "We connect to the land and draw energy out of its abundance of good energy", but: it is ours to tend, and mend the place.

I find that noteworthy, and worthy to spread, to western people, at least. It is not only about coming back to connecting to the land, that is where it starts, but it has to go on to really doing something for the land too. Energetically. And physically too. Doing a real exchange.

Rotger Heilmeier, Systemic Constellation Facilitator, Shamanic Practitioner, Homeopath

https://jester-counseling.com

Ancestral Indigenous Reconnection: A Sacred Weaving of Mystical Spirituality, Embodiment Practices, and Nature Constellations
By Rani George

Ancestral lines lead back, at some point in time, to where our people were indigenous to the land they lived on and deeply connected to nature and spirit. Many of us, through ancestral experiences of the trauma of immigration, war, famine, genocide, slavery, natural disasters, and other personal or collective events, may have been disconnected from that natural resourcing. In North America in particular, except for the Native Peoples, the rest of us have come from "somewhere else". That point of separation from the land of our people was often a severing. The way of survival in the new land often meant dissociation from family, culture, language, and foods. The mountains, rivers, trees and medicinal herbs that resourced our people appeared to be no longer available. Looking back was often too painful and assimilating into our place in the melting pot became the guiding goal. It doesn't matter how many generations back the severing might have been, the trauma can still be alive in our bodies.

I would like to share some of my personal story as an example of how various threads have been woven into an evolving form of Nature Constellations. It grew out of the understanding that our bodies hold both the deep memories of the trauma of leaving home and the further back resource of our indigeneity. Embodied meditative travel into an Inner Knowing Field came to allow reconnection with the love and wisdom of our well-resourced ancient ones. The elements of nature that sustained them are available to us still. Those elements can also be brought into conscious relation with those of the land we currently reside on.

A Family Story

I was born in Kerala, India a decade after independence from Britain. I was home-birthed on my maternal ancestral property, a precious estate named "Fieldland". My mother was one of eight sisters, I was one of twenty first cousins and my grandparents nurtured a multigenerational haven we have all called home at some point or the other. My father was the youngest, by many years, with 3 elder sisters who he had not really grown up with and a brother who had died in his 20's. The family was agrarian, and my memories of that home have more to do with the land than the people. My parents ended up immigrating to the United States for higher education when I was two years old. I have no conscious memory of that time but have heard many stories of my heartbreak and longing to be back on that land with those people. We travelled often during my childhood to visit India and a strong connection with those roots was maintained. One aspect I particularly treasure is the continuation of a strong lineage of spiritual practices. Participating in the daily family prayers was sometimes resisted but was not optional. I was always grateful in the end that I was included. I clearly remember the energetic shift in the room when the prayers began. We collectively dipped into a shared multi-generational mystical container. The melodious recitation in Sanskrit-based Malayalam (the language of Kerala) enveloped us in the holding of ancient sacred lineages. I may not have had words for the experience then, but I knew we were held by something greater than ourselves and felt the rhythmic movement through my body. These practices grounded me and have continued to support and deepen my experiential connection with the Divine all through my life. I honor my parents, their parents, and the multitude of mothers and fathers before them who have kept these practices alive. Always drawn to sacred spaces and practices throughout my childhood and adolescence, I have settled into a daily meditation practice now for over four decades. This includes a blend of mantra repetition, visualizations, rosary recitation, yogic embodiment practices, breath work, and more.

An interesting integration of various spiritual practices from different traditions was actually made possible with immigration held in the Universal Indigenous Field. I find that integration to have some significance regarding connection between land of origin and land of settling. My family, maternal and paternal, belong to an ancient Catholic community called Syro-Malabar Christians. It is believed that St. Thomas, the apostle, came to southern India around 50 A.D., established several communities, and is buried there. Our family is believed to have descended from one of those original communities. This community has always been a minority within the Hindu majority. As such, there may have been strict restrictions to participating in Hindu spiritual practices. However, I believe that the deeper sacred impulse at the origin of both religions as earth-based spiritualities continued to feed the community as underground rivers of wisdom.

My mother was a channel for some of that to emerge. As a young woman she felt called to enter the convent as a Catholic nun. She ended up being persuaded to choose marriage. After arriving in the United States, her deep spirituality led her to explore yoga and meditation. She would not have been oriented or able to pursue that as a Catholic of her generation in India. In her new land, that avenue of reconnection with her indigenous ancestral practices was opened.

She then found her way to various pioneers of Christian/ Hindu dialogue who had begun ashrams in India dedicated to the Wisdom lineages of both religions. She invited and ushered me into those explorations and then her grandchildren were brought in. At one point, we had three generations of adults born in different lands, alive and immersed in these mystical practices together for at least a decade. I realized through explorations in the Field that even in the presence of colonization, fighting for independence, and immigration, unseen threads had been woven into a sacred tapestry that held us. She had been guided through the knowing field of her own indigenous lineage. Without a single day of "training", she was a brilliant facilitator!

One foundation for holding all these experiences in the Field was my 30-year practice as a hands-on energy healing practitioner and teacher. This is another essential thread of the fabric of this reconnection process. My initiation into that realm began on Indian soil while on vacation there from the U.S. My mother and I were cross pollinating our two lands and spiritualities. While in meditation, I experienced a deep spiritual awakening with the body very much included. It was profound and little unsettling. Yet, I trusted it because it arose out of prayer. I was guided to a local practitioner, who suggested that I was an emerging healer. I was not aware at that time of such a calling but continued to be guided even as I returned to the U.S. It was after I had become established as a practitioner and teacher of the healing arts for 10 years that I came across Systemic Constellations.

I knew the first moment that I represented in a constellation that this was for me. The following week, ancestors of my clients started showing up energetically in my treatment room and I knew I needed more guidance on this path. I did a two-year training in Family Systems Constellations with Joanne Lynch Bachbauer and gratefully integrated this work into my practice.

It was almost 5 years later that Nature Constellations entered my awareness in a new way. This awareness came in the form of Francesca Mason Boring on faculty at the North American Intensive in Connecticut in 2012. I sensed as soon as we met that she would be my guide for a new direction that my work in Systemic Constellations would take.

She shared how when she first experienced a Constellation process, she recognized it immediately as the ceremony and ritual of her Native American Shoshone people. She knew instinctively how to navigate the terrain and there was no question of trusting the work. The gift she ultimately offered me was not to learn about the Shoshone ways of accessing knowing but a slow delving into the ways of my own people and their indigeneity to the land they lived on. I sensed that there was some potential, deep reconnection calling me to bring more authenticity to my unique access to the Knowing Field. I was being guided on my sacred path in the Universal Indigenous Field.

Fairly soon after this meeting I began organizing workshops and trainings for in Maryland on the east coast of the U.S. My daughter supported me with that and began her training as a facilitator. Another generation was consciously engaging with the Field.

In time, she and I began offering monthly constellation workshops as mother and daughter together. They were called

Yoga Constellations and later Body Constellations emphasizing the focus on the body as nature and the sacred container through which we access the Field. Utilizing the sacred practices from our lineage allowed a unique access to the Field. Participants often said that just being in Circle with a mother/ daughter facilitator team brought healing.

We offered our workshops in a yurt we built in our backyard in Maryland. Even that process was held in the Field. Immediately after completing the building, I had a strong experience on entering it. I was enveloped in the sounds, smells, and sights of India. Not only India in general but specifically Kerala. This lasted for many months, and I took the mysterious experience as an invitation and a blessing to immerse myself in awareness of the natural world of my ancestry. Then, one day, I entered the yurt, and it was Maryland! The land I had lived on for over 50 years was opening to me in a profound new way. The Universal Indigenous Field had held the two fields in communion and invited us into new dimensions of experiencing "home".

The Indigenous Ancestral Reconnection process has been offered in various formats:

One-on-one in person and on-line. This allows for a very personal process to unfold in its own pace and time.

In person and on-line with small groups of 2-6 people. There is an intimacy that evolves in these groups. The shared process of invoking and being present to each other's ancient ancestors and the gifts they offer bring a different depth of experience.

In person and on-line for conferences, intensives, and workshops with groups ranging in size from 30 to 200 participants. This allows individual process to be supported and enhanced by collective processes. It also gives greater opportunity to enhance the meditative process with small group constellation exercises to further explore what the ancestors or the land have offered each seeker.

The sessions have been either singular experiences to find what's ready to be shown, a series of 2-3 sessions to explore the relationship between land of birth or ancestry and land of current residence, or a series of 4-5 sessions to explore resourcing available in each of the 4 major biological lineages.

The structure or elements of a Reconnection session are varied, with some essential common aspects:

Time for sharing of known family history

An opening ritual

Guided process for fuller embodiment

Intuitive body scanning and connection process

Guided meditation/visualization constellations in the Universal Indigenous Field

Honoring and gratitude ritual to close

Time for integration and further exploration if possible.

It became clearer to me that there had been a gradual evolution in my awareness of the role of healing modalities in my life. A subtle movement from primarily using them as interventions for a specific issue in a mostly psychotherapeutic way, to a deeper awareness of walking in the Field as a spiritual way of life. Connection to my spiritual indigeneity had begun to transcend the location I lived in or which religion I called my own. I had come to an understanding of my body as a sacred container connecting me to all the bodies who came before me. I was opening to a process that allowed me to accompany others to this connection with their own well-resourced ancient ancestors who had lived in good relationship with the natural world. Indigenous Ancestral Reconnection has been the process that has allowed me to walk with many on this sacred path.

This respectful interaction can give us deeper permission to more fully inhabit our bodies and the land we live on. There is also the invitation to engage with the indigenous spirituality of our people before religion, patriarchy, colonization, and rupture from the honoring of Mother Earth. We may walk differently in life when this happens.

Bio:

Rani George, after her academic training and work as a chemist, entered the world of energy therapy almost 35 years ago beginning with training in homeopathy, followed by many body-based energy modalities.

A Family and Systems Constellations facilitator; she has trained with numerous Masters in the field and has completed and organized multiple Constellation Facilitator Trainings with Francesca Mason Boring. She is certified as a hospice companion and serves as a teacher and mentor for complimentary modalities in that field. A certified mantra meditation teacher and a graduate of Thomas Hubel's Timeless Wisdom Training, her current work person and on-line focuses on the integration of systemic constellations, hands-on energy healing for embodiment, and mystical spiritual practices. She offers private and group facilitation, both in-person and on-line.

circlefolks@aol.com
www.circlefolks.com

Pet Constellations: Our interface with the four-legged and more

In many Native American Circles, a prayer is summarized by saying "All My Relations." This is both a blessing and an honoring: *I wish all my relations well, and I hold the hope that all of my relations will be proud of me and judge me as able to live well beside them.* This statement affirms our understanding that we are not separate from nature; we are connected, in fact, we are all relatives: the two legged, the four legged, the six legged, the eight legged, and everything that swims, crawls and flies. We are also connected to the land and all the elements; these are our relatives as well.

When first introduced to family system constellations I was aware that in most forms of western influenced healing modalities animals were excluded, or diminished greatly. It was also apparent that slowly, slowly, western paradigms were opening to remember the connection that man had always had with animals. Family systems constellation initially was focused on the family of origin and happily included ancestors. There was a glimmer of hope that this work could include our whole family. The expansion of the definition and perception of family when the 'field' came into play, and the focus became the family 'system' was encouraging.

It was natural in this methodology, to include the resources, the beloved, the totality of who we belonged to and with.

Family Constellation is a method which has utilized the 'knowing field' so named by Albrecht Mahr (Ritter, L., 2020), to reveal and describe the energy field within family systems and the representative perception which could clarify hidden dynamics within systems. Originally the work was applied to family systems, but the work, like a spring thaw, has grown as our inhibitions and awareness of our self-limiting paradigms melt with greater exposure to the impact and potential of this work.

One of the most legendary and documented evidences of this field phenomena which connects across time and space is the relationship between humans and animals.

Rupert Sheldrake (Sheldrake, R., 2011) shared various research examples of our connection to our four-legged friends. One of the phenomena that was examined was the experience that many pet owners share, the faithful dog waiting by the door when we arrive at our home. What was not expected was that in fact, the dog went to the door the moment the human put on their coat to leave for home. Whether the human came from a different direction, varied their time of departure, or traveled in a different vehicle, the dog was at the ready from the moment the human was actually prepared to leave for home.

Bobbie the Wonder Dog traveled 2,800 miles in the winter to reunite with his human family in 1924. The Oregon Humane Society researched the journey and numerous letters confirmed the route of the dog. The number of stories of similar occurrences are too numerous to mention. (Stelljes, S., 2018)

Admittedly, I have a bias. I learned to ride horseback on the same dapple gray farm horse who taught my mother to ride.

Gray Dog was the teacher of dozens of cousins. The gilding would walk along the fence to see which of the youngsters was ready, stop to let the little person climb on his wide back, and then slowly walk around until the child was satisfied. For longer trips, Gray Dog would patiently wait with any child who had not properly cinched the saddle, until an adult could restore the saddle and child to our teacher's back.

My first dog was one of my first loves and walked with me for my first 16 years. The love, the smell, and the gift of having a silent, vigilant confidant is still a part of my relational foundation.

Into adulthood I was met with the integrity and bonds of humans and animals.

Living in a rural part of North Eastern Washington State in the United States, if we had need to travel it was important not to leave animals alone for any length of time. We had decided to share our home with a large Newfoundland dog with flowing black coat after learning that his master was unable to continue to keep him. 'Ty' had definitely started out with love. He was playful, loyal and smart.

We had neighbors who were willing to dog sit while we took a short trip one winter. The neighbor's home was full of children. Some had special needs, all provided a human blanket of excitement when our big dog came to visit.

Our winters are usually snowy, and can be quite cold, sometimes below zero, requiring the respect of both dog and man. When we returned home after a few days to retrieve our companion the mother in the home said she had so much enjoyed 'Ty' being there, and to our surprise she became tearful. She assured us that it was nothing bad and she recounted an event during Ty's stay.

Apparently, the children wanted to go out to play in the snow. There were a half dozen children, and they had grown up with our crispy winters, so the mother bundled them up with strict instructions, "Take Ty with you and keep your coats on!" Some 15 minutes later she heard a persistent scratch on the door and barking. She was a little startled and opened the door to look down and see Ty with one of the little children's coats in his mouth. She looked out and could not see the children. They had all gone to the other side of the barn out of view, and were sledding sans coats, even the smallest child (who unknowingly provided the evidence). The mother wept with gratitude because she said she truly felt that 'Ty' was an angel, who had watched over the children with an intelligence that moved her.

I don't think I need to tell you where Ty lived out the rest of his days, much to the delight of all the children and the relief of the mother. Our consolation was in knowing that we had at least a small part in finding the place where Ty was called to serve.

It has touched my heart when clients who have lost a spouse subsequently suffer the death of a companion animal. Stories of animal heroics and dogs or cats traveling hundreds, even thousands of miles alone to reunite with families who had to move suddenly, have always been a very real testament of the transcendence of some of the bonds that can exist between an animal and a human.

In constellation work there are so many supports for separation and loss. It seemed only appropriate to offer that support to clients who were depressed by the loss of such a vital part of their support system when an animal companion dies. It is helpful to consider that some dogs provide companionship for 20+ years, and horses can be loved by the same human for

30+ years. These timelines are longer than many marriages last, longer than most children stay in the home. These relationships are significant, and I dare say, constitute a soul connection in many instances.

Dr. Edward Beltran, DVM of Ottawa, Canada was one of the first veterinarians to include the use of systems constellation in the holistic treatment of animals and his consistency can serve as a beacon for those who wonder about the relevance of this application of systemic constellation work.

The following are some scenarios in which a constellation can be helpful to the client:

- **The goodbye**: When there is a pet who is dying, it is helpful to place a constellation to allow the animal to speak. One may call it a ritual constellation, but given the field phenomenon there are times that the statements of the animal are particularly poignant and resound with a specific truth of their relationship to their human.
- **Multiple pets in conflict with each other**: When one has more than one animal and there seems to be constant friction between them, it can be helpful to actually set up the pets. It has been effective to first provide a constellation which clarifies primacy. If it has not been acknowledged who came first, sometimes there is a tension in an unconscious struggle for hierarchy. If the owner witnesses and the representative for the pets in conflict acknowledge which one came first, there has been consistent feedback from clients that the conflicts diminish.

There are times when it becomes apparent that the symptoms are being carried for the human, or serve as a distraction from the pain (physical or emotional) off the human.

- **When a pet has chronic health issues** place representatives for:

The owner
The pet
The illness

In one constellation for a service animal who had witnessed a traumatic event, the dog was available to be present. He sat and watched the whole of the constellation attentively as he was represented, and we were also able to honor his parents who had also spent their lives in public service.

When a pet has been traumatized, or is unstable, place representatives for the healthy ancestors of the representative for the pet behind the representative of the animal.

As we become more conscious and whole, it is easier to be aware of the other. Among the many beings that we share the planet with, our pets are some we hold most dear.

They literally serve as eyes and ears for those who do not have sight or hearing. They are nannies and companions for widows and widowers.

Being comfortable, as a facilitator to support pet owners, four legged relatives and others can be a balm for the soul for those who are experiencing challenges. Perhaps most promising, representing an animal who loves a human being, can open the heart to the possibility of unconditional love and our own capacity for bonds and affection.

Two Significant Constellations
By Barbara Morgan

I have had many amazing experiences communing with Nature over the years: Some of them profoundly moving; others rather entertaining. I could write a whole chapter on my experiences but one of the most significant I had was prior to leaving my previous house here in Frome, Somerset in the United Kingdom. Mostly I soon forget the constellations I do, but these two stood out for me as they were significant in how my life moved forward afterwards.

First Constellation:

Background

I had been in my house around 8 years and loved it. I had a large garden with seven raised beds, a greenhouse, three compost bins and accompanying creatures.

The year before I left my house it began to be 'invaded' by some of these creatures and plants. I put the word 'invaded' in inverted commas because it became significant.

The first of the invaders was a squirrel in my loft. I thought it was a rat and immediately called the 'rat catcher'. He told me it was in fact a squirrel and had put down some poison. I didn't feel great about that and was interested that the bushy tail on the squirrel somehow differentiated it from the somewhat maligned rat.

I heard it scuttling about a few times and occasional bumps as it began to collapse. When the rat-catcher returned he couldn't find it and assumed it had escaped from the loft.

A couple of weeks later I had a very strange, unpleasant smell in my hallway, which I thought must be leaking gas. When the gasman arrived he immediately dismissed my concern and said: "That's not gas, it's a rotting corpse. Don't worry open all the doors and windows the smell will disappear in a couple of weeks."

He was right. The smell went and I thought no more about it.

In the meantime, my washing machine suddenly stopped working and when I called the engineer he found the cable chewed through and guessed it might be a rat. Sure enough when I investigated, there were other signs – nothing but shreds left on my tulip bulbs and other trails of droppings. Assuming it had left, I did nothing more about the rat.

Next in line was a family of jackdaws. They had been nesting rather precariously in my chimney and one evening I heard a thud and found the baby sitting looking rather shell-shocked in my fire-grate.

A couple of minutes later another two birds dropped which I presumed to be the mother and father. I called a friend who came and wrapped them in a towel and took them outside.

Alongside these 'invading' creatures, I had two invasive plants: At the front of my house was a mass of bamboo. I couldn't get rid of it and it was beginning to spread into the foundations. I asked a friend to come over with his chainsaw and followed some instructions from the internet to spray each plant with vinegar as soon as it had been cut. It made no difference at all.

Out the back was columbine (also known as bindweed) and relentless pulling it up did nothing to dissuade this plant from continuing to creep throughout my garden and strangle other possibilities of life.

The final straw and the moment when I really got the message that I wasn't wanted in this house anymore, was when I returned one evening to find my large picture windows completely black with flies. Strangely these tiny insects had a far greater impact on me than any of the previous 'invaders'. I became murderous in my attempts to rid my house of them, but I didn't know whether they had come in from outside or were inside trying to get out.

I rang the Department of Health (who I discovered have a section specialising in flies!) They listed many different species and suggested they may be cluster flies and someone would come out and help me get rid of them in 24 hours. I told them I could not wait that long. I was horrified at the thought of sharing my house and my favourite room with these insects!

After a short while another 'expert' rang me and suggested they may have come from a 'hatching' and suddenly the penny dropped! These were from the rotting corpse of the squirrel – blue bottles hatched from the maggots. He suggested opening all the windows and letting them out, which I duly did and they soon disappeared.

On an Intensive at Kloster Bernried in Germany I asked Francesca to facilitate me in a constellation to see what the message was for me from what had been happening in my house.

The first thing she pointed out to me was my use of the word 'invaded'. Somehow it had a systemic resonance. I set up representatives for each of the creatures and received some important messages from each. My first response to the constellation was to say to Francesca: "I don't think these representatives are taking this seriously." Her response was: "What do you expect? They're creatures!"

I don't remember all the messages – from the rats it was to be at home more because if I didn't heed the message, they would return.

I think it was the jackdaws who delivered a message from my father.

But what stood out most was the representative for my bamboo who I hadn't noticed until the moment she spoke, was wearing a teeshirt with a bamboo image on it. She said she felt like a woman waiting for her lover to come home. Two representatives began humming the Skye Boatsong (Skye is an island off the coast of Scotland)[2].

The constellation ended and I was reflecting on it over coffee afterwards. Francesca suggested lining up some cups and glasses on the table and underneath she placed pieces of paper with 50, 100, 200, over 200 years ago written on them and then asked me to choose one. I chose over 200 years ago.

That night she had a dream which she reported to me the following day. She'd had an image of the Union Jack[1] which had no significance for her and she thought may have some relevance for me. I looked it up and saw that back in 1606 King James VI of Scotland became King of England and ordered the Scottish and English ships to join together and create one flag – the Union Jack. There was a battle between the ships carrying these different flags, prior to the unification.

I can never know for sure, but I was left wondering whether an ancestor of mine had in fact been on one of those ships and maybe invaded one of the islands off the coast of England or Scotland. Maybe the lover, the representative of bamboo was waiting for this man to return home.

Second Constellation:

The second constellation of significance for me took place at a workshop in Bristol facilitated by Zita Cox. I explained how indignant I had been when 'my hill' (a hill I had climbed almost every day of my childhood) was now fenced off and designated 'an area of outstanding natural beauty' restricting my ability to wander freely over the land. The second piece was that every time I saw a meadow or even an image of one, I cried. These meadows had had great significance for me as a child. I had gone there to lie down on the grass right in the midst of the most beautiful wild flowers, surrounded by bees and butterflies and they had all but disappeared in the UK. I had felt such a depth of peace when lying there.

I told Zita I didn't know which of these two pieces to choose and she suggested both. So we went outside and picked one area of land to represent 'my hill' (called 'Camels' Hump' by the locals) and a separate patch to represent 'meadows'. I began in the one representing meadows and one of the representatives closely resembled my mother. I made a tearful connection to her and to the meadows, which had so nourished me in my childhood.

We then processed from there to the other piece of land, which seemed to in some way resemble my father. (As I say that, I recall that my father and I had had one of the most profound sharings of my life sitting on that hill and we were both so engrossed we failed to notice that a herd of cows had surrounded us completely – almost as if they were protecting us.)

I don't recall much else from the constellation but I went straight from the workshop to 'my hill' and there to my complete delight I saw that to the right of the path a beautiful wildflower meadow was developing. These two separate images from my childhood (representing my mother and father) had somehow come together.

I sat for some time absorbing this new image, completely lost in the awe of it and literally skipped back down 'my' hill afterwards.

When I arrived at the bus stop I realised I had been so engrossed in what was happening I had somehow managed to lose my purse, which I needed for my journey home. A few minutes later I received a phone call from a man who had found it under the stile. He asked where I was and brought it to me. What kindness and what a profound to what had been a truly beautiful day!

As I recall these two events, I am flooded by other memories of nature constellations that have served me over the years and helped inspire my complete faith in our link to all that is and nature as the most profound vehicle for getting in touch with that.

Thank you constellation work, Bert Hellinger, Hunter Beaumont and others, but particularly Francesca Mason Boring for helping bring the profile of Nature Constellations so much to the fore in our work.

I will be eternally grateful to you.

Barbara

Note:

1. The origins of the earlier flag of Great Britain date back to 1606. King James VI of Scotland had inherited the English and Irish thrones in 1603 as James I, thereby uniting the crowns of England, Scotland, and Ireland in a personal union, although the three kingdoms remained separate states. On 12 April 1606, a new flag to represent this regal union between England and Scotland was specified in a royal decree, according to which the flag of England, a red cross on a white background, known as St George's Cross, and the flag of Scotland, a white saltire (X-shaped cross, or St Andrew's Cross) on a blue background, would be joined, forming the flag of England and Scotland for maritime purposes.

The present design of the Union Flag dates from a Royal proclamation following the union of Great Britain and Ireland in 1801. The flag combines aspects of three older national flags: the red cross of St George for the Kingdom of England, the white saltire of St Andrew for Scotland and the red saltire of St Patrick to represent Ireland. Although the Republic of Ireland is no longer part of the United Kingdom, Northern Ireland is.

There are no symbols representing Wales in the flag, making the Principality of Wales the only home nation with no representation, as at the time of the Laws in Wales Acts 1535 and 1542 (creating legal union with England) the concept of national flags was in its infancy. The Welsh Dragon was however adopted as a supporter in the royal coat of arms of England used by the Tudor dynasty from 1485.

2. Skye Boat Song

Sing me a song of a lass that is gone
Say, could that lass be I?
Merry of soul, she sailed on a day
Over the sea to Skye

Billow and breeze, islands and seas
Mountains of rain and sun (mountains of rain and sun)
All that was good, all that was fair
All that was me is gone

Sing me a song of a lass that is gone
Say, could that lass be I?
Merry of soul, she sailed on a day
Over the sea to Skye

Sing me a song of a lass that is gone
Say, could that lass be I?

Bio: Originally trained as a Gestalt Psychotherapist, Barbara Morgan has been working with constellations since 1997, one year after the Founder, Bert Hellinger first came to England. Currently Barbara is training people in the UK and offers Advanced Training in both the UK and Romania. She runs regular workshops online and in person in the UK and Ireland. Barbara works with individuals in Bath (Somerset, UK) or online.

Barbara has been the Editor of The Knowing Field since 2004, and is author of several books, her first being Coming Home: A First step into the World of Family Constellations. She sees Family Constellations as a way of life and her pursuit of 'truth' as far as that is ever possible leads to a deep commitment to the work she does. Second only to family, it is her guiding passion.

https://www.cominghome.org.uk

Notes on "Corona & Mother Earth" Constellation held Thursday, April 9th, 2020
By: Megan Kelly

This Constellation was done with a small group of people during the first of the Covid lockdowns. It was part of an online series of Constellations to explore Covid from different angles, this time from the perspective of nature and Mother Earth. As little was known about Covid at the time, we considered that it could be an airborne virus.

Representatives:
The Virus (later became the Heart)
Mother Earth
The Sky (later Earth Consciousness)
Humankind
Animals (later became Animal Consciousness)
5G

As we opened the constellation, the representative for the Sky slowly went to the ground (like dirt in water settling to the bottom of a bottle) and the representative for Mother Earth squeezed herself from her diaphragm and moved upwards, to the lungs. The representative for Humankind turned to protect herself, like putting herself into defensive mode facing such circumstances. The representative for Animals yawned and was tired, while the representative for 5G looked up to the sky.

5G reported feeling interested in the Virus and connected to the "Sky." 5G looked at Mother Earth and felt sad. "I see she's uncomfortable and in pain," said 5G. Mother Earth looked at 5G and felt another burden. "The earthlings are inventing more toys; they don't know what it will bring, and I'm the one who has to deal with it." Mother Earth looked at Humankind and said "We are hurting each other."

The Sky looked at the Virus and reported him to be poetic, "like a work of art." The Animal kingdom was connected to the Virus. "I feel superior to the Virus," and the Virus responded by saying **"You (animals) are someone I use. You aren't valuable to me. I go there (to the animals) whenever I want."** That's when Mother Earth stepped in to protect the Animals saying, "No, you cannot go wherever you want. I decide where you can go." It was then that the Virus could respect Mother Earth.

The Animals said to the Virus, **"You can't ignore me because you have been created by me**." Again, the Animal Kingdom seemed to feel in control and not controlled by the Virus. "We are more powerful than you think. Now we are going to rest and not serve." Humankind was destabilized hearing this and started to rock from side to side. The Virus didn't agree that the Animals were in control and wanted to laugh seeing them and Humankind demobilized.

Mother Earth felt angry with Humankind and said, "You created this for yourself. Now, deal with it. Why do I have to clean up all the time? **The Virus is helping me to clean up what isn't necessary anymore for human consciousness… this virus is a helper.**" The Virus responded in an arrogant tone and Mother Earth reminded him to be calm and said to humans, "Grow up."

5G had sat down at this point and didn't feel very involved. The Virus was no longer interested in 5G and was humble toward Mother Earth. Mother Earth said to Humankind "This (5G) is a toy you created, so deal with it instead of being angry at me. Learn to play with it in a safe way, but it's your decision what you do with it." 5G reported only feeling like an observer to the scene, not overly involved with anyone anymore. "I'm completely neutral, just watching. I'm interested but just watching (in a passive way)." 5G also reported saying, "There's a deeper knowing" related to the Virus but it didn't come out here and 5G instead felt out of the scene.

The Animal Kingdom was more connected to the Virus than to 5G. The Sky was deeply connected to Mother Earth and was tired of being on its knees. The Sky reported feeling sad how the Virus talked to others saying, "He (the virus) is not connected. He's not connected to the rest, and he doesn't have the consciousness of being one, like I do."

This is when the Sky was the first shift in acknowledging unity to all things.

"I'm connected to all of you. We are one." (From this point on the Sky represented Earth Consciousness instead of the Sky.)

After speaking, the Sky could stand and said, "Now I can breathe." Its focus was then on Humankind. "I look at

Humankind and I feel sad, (as it held its womb)." Mother Earth at this point also held its womb and said, "I'm surprised there is so much consciousness. I see part of the humans who are growing up… they are finding balance. Any change comes from Humankind. **This is a lesson for the human race to open their heart (chakra). Humankind I have a message for you. This is a lesson on opening the heart instead of living in the mind, in the ego and being self-righteous. (Let's let) opening the heart be part of our communication (together)."**

And this was the first of many messages about the heart, first coming from Mother Earth.

Humankind as a result felt more seen and taken care of from this message. The Animals forgot about the Virus at this point and were focused on Humankind as well saying, "Humankind the earth is for you and for me, but you need us more than we need you." Humankind then felt like a "scale" and acknowledged a need to find more balance, "so I can look at things differently."

Then the Virus said to Humankind, "This is the first of three warnings. You should start to do something." Humankind agreed and reported needing direction and not knowing where to turn. "I think we need to be told what to do. We need direction." Mother Earth then said, "I want to tell you what to do." Then the Virus spoke and these were its last words before changing to a different representative: "**Direction is within your heart, to look inside. It's also true you need new leaders.**" (From this point on the Virus representative instead represented the Heart.) Mother Earth was happy her earlier message of the heart was finally heard. She was happy it came through the Virus and she felt her and the Virus could cooperate together. "I feel we (to the Virus) are working together to help Humankind and to raise consciousness for them to protect themselves."

Animals as a result felt even more connected to Mother Earth, but they still felt like humans were arrogant and not needed. Humankind was hurt to hear that from Animals. Mother Earth said, **"Animal consciousness is higher than human consciousness at this moment,"** and Humankind agreed with sadness. (The Animal representative now represented Animal Consciousness.)

The Heart was added to the constellation as a representative and as a result Humankind felt calmer and "more in my own power." Earth Consciousness also felt calmer with the Heart present and told the others, **"The heart is the bridge between the spiritual world and the material world."** Humankind could be humble before Mother Earth with the presence of the heart and Mother Earth said, "I feel proud of Humankind that they're growing. I feel less of a burden now for the Animals." Animal Consciousness also felt closer to humans after these movements. "Before I felt Humankind didn't get it and needed to be more humble, but now I think maybe we can co-exist. I feel hope." With the presence of the heart, Earth Consciousness also went from feeling humans were "lost" to feeling "a deep movement inside of me. This is profound. The advice (about the heart) from the Virus surprises me."

The rest of the parts reported feeling calm, hopeful, proud, awakened and strong.

The message comes from the Heart. With its presence, all the others could be put into order and were more equal.

Highlights:

It was the Sky that could acknowledge unity among all things and all creatures. **"I'm connected to all of you. We are one."**

Mother Earth first spoke of living in the heart: This is a lesson to Humankind on opening the heart instead of living in the mind and in the ego... (Let's let) opening the heart be part of our communication (together)."

After the Virus spoke that there were only 3 warnings, Humankind could humble itself and said, "I think we need to be told what to do. We need direction." The Virus said the direction comes through the heart, echoing what Mother Earth had earlier said. The Virus also acknowledged the need for new leaders.

It was Earth Consciousness who said, **"The heart is the bridge between the spiritual world and the material world."**

Acknowledging a need for help and humility from the part of Humankind, a shift could happen and parts in the field became more equal. It was then that animals reported feeling compassion for humans and feeling more equal too. "I feel we can cohabitate."

5G was considered a "human toy" that Mother Earth would have to deal with. It had some connection to the virus and reported a "deeper knowing" but it wasn't so relevant for this constellation and we weren't able to get more information from the Field at this time on this subject.

The Virus seemed to have more connection to Animals instead of 5G, even saying in the beginning "I go there whenever I want." Animals in response said to the Virus, "You can't ignore me as I created you."

The topic of 5G with the virus and on health could be further explored. For the intention of this constellation, it was the least important role.

Reflections from Meghan:

Many things stood out to me during this constellation, including the wisdom of the Animal kingdom and their relation to Humankind, the realization that we are all one under the same sky, and the initial image of Mother Earth squeezing herself and moving upward to the lungs, much like the conditions of our world and how the lungs of the Earth are at risk and are being squeezed. The image of Mother Earth squeezing herself is also symbolic of what was happening during Covid for people all over the world. Each person was being squeezed and challenged in a way they hadn't been before, showing our direction relation with Mother Earth.

Bio: Meghan Kelly, a Systemic Constellation Facilitator & Integrative Therapist, was born and raised in Colorado in the United States who as an adult followed the path of her ancestors back to Europe. Today she is based in Brussels, Belgium and serves the international community as well as a larger community online. With more than ten years of experience in accompanying others, today as an Integrative Therapist Meghan combines Constellation work with other tools including Systemic Ritual®, Psychosomatic Bodywork & Trauma Recovery and Developmental Astrology. Her approach is an integral one that includes the whole person - body, mind and spirit .

Meghan is passionate about sharing Constellations with others for healing, understanding and accessing the greater mystery of life and our family stories. Her approach to Constellation work has been inspired by the wide range of teachers she's had in different countries and cultures and in particular Systemic Ritual, which brings together elements of Family Constellations and shamanic ritual. She first discovered Constellations and Shamanism while living in Latin America (Argentina) for many years. Today this connection with Spirit and shamanic practices is a part of her everyday

meghan@gettotheorigin.com
www.gettotheorigin.com

Nature Constellations and The Work that Reconnects
By Matthew Ramsay, M.SC., P.Ag, RTC

So the story goes: Siddhartha Gautama was seated beneath an ancient fig tree when he was assailed by the forces of Mara (the tempter) trying to dissuade him from continuing his spiritual quest to realize the end of suffering. He remained resolute throughout temptations of seduction and provocation and then the final challenge from Mara came in the form of a question along the lines of: "*who do you think you are, sitting there thinking you can achieve enlightenment*!? *...that seat belongs to me* (Mara), *as witnessed by my legions of forces ...who will speak for you*?" Famously, Siddhartha wordlessly reached out his right hand and touched the Earth, and the Earth shook and spoke, "I bear witness to you!" Mara vanished and as the morning star shone in the sky, Siddhartha realized enlightenment and became a Buddha. To this day, this story is encapsulated within Buddhist iconography in statutes and artwork whenever you see the Buddha-touching-earth-mudra (hand gestures that convey both symbolic and experiential functions). In this story, we see a reference to Nature as an inner resource for human beings that is at least 2,500 years old and from a particular cultural/spiritual tradition. Without a doubt, there are similar examples of this relationship on each continent, across varied cultures, and extending even farther back in time. Therefore, the idea and experience of Nature as an inner resource (versus as a material resource, only), has been with us for a long time and for many people it continues to be so, both in life at large, and within the practice of systemic constellations work (SCW) - particularly Nature Constellations.

The confluence of four streams that have contributed to the emergence of Nature Constellations is described in the introduction to Returning to Membership in Earth Community: Systemic Constellations with Nature (Mason Boring & Sloan, Eds 2013). Within the particular stream of Deep Ecology is the specific tributary currently known as, the Work That Reconnects, established by Joanna Macy and colleagues. The introduction to Mason Boring & Sloan (2013) describes one of the experiential group processes of the Work That Reconnects, called the Council of All Beings, which is quite similar in form and experience to SCW with its use of representatives (including both human and non-human). The Work That Reconnects also integrates a number of streams, two of which include Buddhism and General Systems Theory (Macy & Brown, 2014). In practice, Buddhism, like SCW, can be viewed as essentially a phenomenological process of observing what emerges through our subjective sensory experience, which often provides a direct embodied experience of our profound interrelatedness with all beings, while holding the awareness of a provisional self-identity and body at the same time. Similarly, General Systems Theory, like SCW, provides a way of seeing ourselves as holons, simultaneously wholes in our own right, and inextricable parts of nested hierarchies (systems within systems). With such theoretical and experiential foundations (i.e., streams) in common among the Work That Reconnects and SCW, there is a great opportunity to integrate more elements of each practice with one another, particularly using Nature Constellations.

While integrating Nature Constellations within the framework of the Work That Reconnects, we can see aspects of the Orders of Love from SCW illuminated and experience Nature as inner resource within each station of the Work That Reconnects process. The Work That Reconnects, like many developmental process-based models, is conceived of as a spiral form since participants can potentially visit four identified stations of the framework repeatedly, each time from a new vantage point over time. It is also represented as a spiral since each station prepares the ground for the station that follows. The Work That Reconnects is essentially a collection of experiential group processes intended to support the emergence, development, and sustaining of all three aspects of the Great Turning towards a more life-sustaining society for all beings on Earth. The three dimensions of the Great Turning represent the spheres of action that are required to support a shift in collective human beliefs and behaviour commensurate with the scale of multiple intersecting social and environmental challenges present at this time in history. These three dimensions include:

1. actions that slow the rate and extent of damage to the Earth and our shared social fabric,
2. systemic change to institutions (such as economic, agricultural, educational, judicial, political, healthcare, etc.),
3. shifting our individual and collective consciousness from the view of self as a body and mind separate from the rest of life, towards one of fundamental awareness of our true nature as profoundly interconnected with life in its many forms and processes.

Any one of these dimensions without the other two is not likely to be sufficient to support the collective shift that is the ultimate aim of the Great Turning; working on all three levels simultaneously is necessary. The Spiral of the Work That Reconnects provides a framework for the progression of experiential group exercises intended to address each dimension of the Great Turning, which cumulatively have the potential to liberate mental an emotional constrictions/blocks, deepen and widen our sense of belonging, and strengthen our resolve to bring forth compassionate action. Nature Constellations provide a fitting process to incorporate within each station of the Spiral. The four stations of the Spiral of the Work That Reconnects are referred to as:

- gratitude
- honouring our pain (for the world)
- seeing with new/ancient eyes
- going forth

The practice of gratitude is often the starting point for a given round of the Spiral because it bolsters our resilience when we recognize how profoundly we receive life. That resilience is often helpful as we prepare to open more fully to the second station of the process: honouring our pain. Gratitude strengthens our resolve to contribute to the Great Turning in the context of balancing giving and receiving life. In this sense, gratitude is more than an emotion we may feel; it is a spiritual practice and orientation. Numerous cultures have traditions of acknowledging the gift of life in its many forms as an opening to ritual and ceremony, or even as the entirety of a particular ritual and ceremony. Nature Constellations (and SCW, more broadly) can certainly take the form of ritual and ceremony in this way as well.

One way to frame the inquiry question of a Nature Constellation process that invites an experience of gratitude in this way is to ask: "*what elements of nature support your (i.e., individual/personal, or collective human) life*?" After generating a number of elements either as a group or working with an individual client, some or all of them can be selected as representatives and placed in the field along with a representative for either the client's personal self, or a representative for humans-collectively, depending on the original intention of the process and group size (this example can be scaled to working with one focal client, in small groups, or as a large group process). Working phenomenologically, the process unfolds organically and the facilitator works with what arises in the field –there is no guarantee that gratitude-as-a-feeling will necessarily arise, nor is the intention to instill this feeling if that is not the authentic experience of the representatives. However, the process offers an opportunity for gratitude to arise and be experienced in a manner that goes beyond one's ideas of it, towards an experience of it in one's own heart, soul, body, belly, and bones. There is the possibility to experientially deepen the cognitive awareness of our profound relational mutuality with fellow aspects of life; this may occur as the client, representative for the client, a witness to the process, or as any one of the elements of nature being represented. Forms familiar to facilitators and practitioners of SCW can spontaneously be incorporated here, such as bowing– not only as a gesture of profound gratitude and respect, but as acknowledgement of who or what came first in the natural order and our respective place in that order individually or collectively; or healing statements that respectfully acknowledge 'what is' and evoke truths that oftentimes run beneath the level of language or thought except during such ceremonial time.

The experience of remaining connected to unconditional gratitude while also connected to deep grief (or other so-called dark emotions) is an expansive one for those that have experienced it. This seeming paradox shows up in SCW with families where there have been both painful or even traumatic experiences, as well as the transmission of life and love too. Holding such dynamic tension within the container of SCW often supports the presence of dignity, respect, and compassion - for both self and other. In the movement from the gratitude-station of the Work That Reconnects to the honouring-of-our-pain-station, quite often an awareness of gratitude goes with us and is even deepened as we honour what we regard as both precious and in peril. In the honouring-our-pain-station of the Work That Reconnects, this pain may include a wide range of feelings: grief, for sure, but also potentially fear, worry, anger, guilt, shame, despair, or even numbness (dissociation, or absence of feeling). The *honouring* part of this station recognizes that when we connect our apparently-personal experience of suffering with the apparently-impersonal pain of the world, this opens up the possibility to enlarge our understanding of our suffering and our sense of self. This movement supports the realization of self-compassion and great-compassion.

Nature can act as resource in this process of honouring our pain for the world in a number of different ways. First, elements of Nature can serve as the focal point of our concern if we perceive their peril (i.e., danger of losing the ability to continue to support life), for example: threatened or endangered species at risk of extinction, or water bodies that have received toxic by-products of industrial pollution. Secondly, elements of nature can serve as witness to the system, even while being a part of it, similar to the Earth in the story of Buddha's earth-touching-mudra. In this example, elements of nature sometimes contribute a somewhat unsentimental perspective born of their long-enduring qualities and unique perspective, which turns out to be grounding, stabilizing, and a fresh perspective alongside the human (or non-human) emotions expressed in this same station of the process. Mountains, for example, have endured the powerful or even violent forces of change present in such activities as tectonic plates thrusting, colliding and rising up or volcanoes erupting – such experiences sometimes place the scale and degree of anthropocentric impacts into a much larger perspective. Perhaps surprisingly, rather than resulting in resignation, encounters with mountains' perspectives can help calm anxiety so effective ameliorative actions at the human scale can proceed rather than be frozen in a trauma response to fear. Thirdly, elements of nature can serve as a resource by sharing their unique qualities. These qualities are sometimes understood symbolically or metaphorically by the interpretive human mind and perspective, (e.g., mountains standing for enduring strength; water bodies standing for the kind of flexibility and adaptability only a fluid could possibly attain, etc.), yet in Nature Constellations such qualities can be apprehended immediately, viscerally, by representatives and witnesses alike. The spectrum of potential qualities of natural elements that could serve as a resource in any situation is as vast as the cosmos itself and as innumerable as all beings on earth throughout space and time. In this sense, Nature-as-resource is truly unlimited, or limited only by our creativity and openness to accessing it in this way.

One way to explore Nature-as-resource in these three ways is to begin with an inquiry from the point of view of a specific client (either individually or a collective group of people) that is holding a concern about a specific element of nature that is in peril or it could also be a social issue characterized by such peril (e.g., past and/or present genocidal practices or policies that threaten the health and survival of certain indigenous communities). When working in a group, potential concerns can be illuminated initially using open sentences from the Work That Reconnects processes such as, "*what concerns me most about the world today is...*" (or derivations thereof). Once representatives for client and concern are placed in the field, reports from the client and/or their representative provide an opportunity for their pain for the world to be acknowledged, expressed, and witnessed. The representative of the client and concern may well need a resource to support this process, and so, complementary elements of Nature can be invited and placed into the field as a resource. Identifying the elements of Nature to serve as resource could arise spontaneously among the representatives, the actual client, the facilitator, witnesses to the constellation, or some combination of the above according to each unique facilitator's approach. Elements of Nature-as-resource could be identified from among the elements identified in the previous exercise about gratitude, or they could be identified during an intervening period of reflection perhaps while walking outdoors. For some people, the knowledge of which elements of Nature are a resource for them has been with them lifelong, so it is more a matter of remembering and calling forth what is already known in one's depths – these elements may have connections to the land or waters of our birthplace or to those of our ancestors. Here is where the qualities of creativity and openness can be so helpful.

Some of the intentions related to inviting such a resource into the constellation include the following: Oftentimes people can allow more of their painful feelings into awareness when there is an empathic other bearing witness to their process. The invitation to acknowledge, express, and have-witnessed one's feelings of pain for the world can provide a different (liberating) experience compared to messages contained in mass media or dominant culture to distract, deny, repress, and/or keep quiet about such feelings and thoughts. When acknowledgement and expression of such pain is shared within a group where support is present, it can counteract the sense that we are alone with such potentially overwhelming feelings, which in-turn can promote healing of individual and/or collective trauma. With the support of Nature-as-resource, it is possible to gain a perspective that the very pain being shared is evidence of deep care, concern, compassion, and ultimately intimate connection, of our profound interrelatedness with other people and other forms of life. The overall intention of the process is not to 'fix' the client's pain, for it is not seen as a pathology to be remedied, but rather the intention, particularly of Nature-as-resource in this instance, is more simply to bear witness and support the experience of pain for the world as it is allowed to surface within a supportive context.

As with the Nature Constellation process described above related to gratitude, the Constellation within the honouring-our-pain-station proceeds organically and incorporates familiar forms adapted from SCW where appropriate.

The potential shift from viewing suffering as a personal problem or affliction to seeing it as both an aspect of a widespread shared experience and as stemming from our intimate connection with life is already an experience of seeing with new eyes – the next station on the Spiral of the Work That Reconnects.

To see with *new* eyes refers to the third aspect of the Great Turning: to experience a shift of consciousness, perspective, and concomitant values. The reference to seeing with *ancient* eyes, in this context is not a reference to previously held limited views, but rather is an acknowledgement that what for some may be experienced as an eye-opening paradigm shift, is how it has always been since time immemorial for others -such as intact traditional cultures - and so not really a *new* perspective at all but rather a return to *ancient* wisdom. In some areas of scientific inquiry, modern discoveries confirm the ancient wisdom of traditional knowledge and so *new* and *ancient* occasionally converge and coexist in our current time. Systemic Constellations Work and Nature Constellations in particular, are the quintessence of this station on the Spiral of the Work That Reconnects. More precisely, the experience of representative consciousness, so readily available through SCW and Nature Constellations, is the very epitome of seeing with new/ancient eyes for it is a whole body-mind-spirit encounter with perspectives larger than our habitual way of seeing self, other, and the world.

This seeing with new/ancient eyes station of the Spiral of the Work That Reconnects often entails two dimensions of new perspectives: one is a re-experiencing, re-imagining, a wider sense of *self-identity*; the other is a re-experiencing, re-imagining a wider sense of *time*; and sometimes these two work together synergistically. Nature Constellations not only provide opportunities to experience a wider sense of self through participation as a representative in the constellation, (particularly of non-human elements), but also, as in SCW applications for family systems that include generations of ancestors, they provide opportunities to directly experience an entirely different scale of time than the one we typically inhabit day to day. In the Work That Reconnects, these processes are called, 'Deep Time' work, and similar to SCW applications for family systems, can include direct encounters with beings of the past, present, and future generations.

Expanding the view of time further to include the evolutionary scale, the notion of ancestors can be expanded to include our non-human predecessors as well. From the perspective of evolutionary biology, these beings of Nature brought forth resources that make us who and what we are today, replete with the miracles of a vascular system, spinal column, nervous system, instinctual brain stem, limbic brain, and opposable digits on our hands. Seeing ourselves as current expressions of one life force continuously evolving into novel forms, it is possible to experience our sense of belonging within an even wider system than that of our family, community, or nation, and we can potentially perceive and acknowledge who came first in temporal and developmental order. Including Nature-as-resource into SCW through Nature Constellations provides an opportunity to see and experience our self-identity and time with new/ancient eyes.

One way to frame an exploration of Deep Time within a Nature Constellation that potentially illuminates Nature-as-resource is to invite representatives of our earliest ancestors from the perspective of evolutionary biology extending back hundreds of millions of years including the worm, fish, amphibians, lizard, rodents, primates, and hominids (this list could also include even earlier stages of life on earth; however this list was selected for their particular anatomical parts and associated functions evident in present day human bodies; this concept is adapted from Work That Reconnects exercises from Brown & Macy (2014)). As in a structural approach to a human family system in SCW (as compared to a purely phenomenological approach), the starting point for this process is a chronological line-up that physicalizes relationships that span great expanses of time. In family systems constellations processes, it is common to acknowledge that life is received (most-immediately) from our biological parents and oftentimes clients experience this acknowledgement of relationship, belonging, and embrace of life as strengthening and supportive; so here too is an opportunity to acknowledge how life has been received from our evolutionary ancestors, potentially providing a dramatically expanded sense of place within the natural order. Whereas human beings are often regarded as the pinnacle of the evolutionary process, this form of Nature Constellation emphasizes the perspective from SCW of the natural hierarchy flowing from those that came first to those that came later, along with the respect, humility, and gratitude that this perspective conveys. In this sense, the balance of giving and receiving is intimated, setting the stage for the next station of the Spiral of the Work That Reconnects: *going forth.*

Through direct encounters with Nature-as-resource in the preceding three stations of the Spiral of the Work That Reconnects, participants will have had the opportunity to recognize how the existence and quality of our human lives (individually and/or collectively) depend upon innumerable beings. Having experienced (or witnessed) qualities of gratitude, acceptance, and belonging within a vast system of relationships, often an impulse towards reciprocity naturally arises or is deepened or renewed. From the perspective of SCW, this relates to the balance of giving and receiving present in relatively more harmonious and flowing systems. In the Work That Reconnects, the fourth station of the Spiral is about going forth, which refers to the ways in which we (individually and collectively) can actively contribute to the Great Turning by giving of our time, talents, and resources in service to life. As a result of the preceding Nature Constellations processes conducted within the framework of the Work That Reconnects, actions pursued within this sphere of going forth have the benefit of being informed by a greater awareness of our relatedness with all beings, greater sensitivity to suffering, a wider sense of community and of time scales. Each of these benefits are amplified by including Nature-as-resource throughout the process.

During the going forth station of the Spiral of the Work That Reconnects, participants often generate ideas of possible initiatives they might pursue and identify steps to strengthen their resolve to follow through on them. They might begin with an intention that aligns with a particular issue or concern that is important to them. Working in small or large group format, options and considerations or constructive action are then explored. One way to incorporate Nature-as-resource in this process is to include the salient elements of a given issue or concern within a Nature Constellation as representatives that can contribute their response to potential actions or solution-oriented strategies as a source of feedback. Given the complexity of systems (natural and/or social), all the contributing causes and conditions influencing any given issue or concern are essentially inconceivable; however, this approach provides feedback that includes elements other than the human perspective and accesses ways of knowing other than just the rational and analytical. It is difficult to list out all the various ways that Nature-as-resource might inform the contemplated action or strategy; instead, these emerge while working phenomenologically. However, one example of the practical implications of this approach on a contemplated action or strategy is to witness the relative influence of select factors on a given issue or concern with the help of feedback from relevant elements of Nature through a Nature Constellation.

In nature, a variety of benefits result from a process called, *hybrid vigor.* This phenomenon is particularly evident when two different varieties of plants are crossed through sexual reproduction; their offspring exhibit traits such as greater stature, abundance, and health, greater resistance to disease, earlier maturation and flowering. Recombination of diverse sources (hybrids) can result in greater vitality (vigor). So, it seems that when two distinct streams of theoretical and experiential approaches flow together, the results can be quite fruitful. This holds true too of the integration of Nature Constellations within the framework of the Work That Reconnects that together illustrate manifold ways that Nature can serve as an inner resource. This description here provides a mere glimpse of the possibilities; there is no substitute for direct experience of this assertion. Taken together, this combination can contribute to our individual and collective participation in the Great Turning towards a more life-sustaining society for all beings on Earth. Within these processes, Nature-as-resource, Earth and all its elements, bears witness to our individual and collective intentions, efforts, commitments, and relatedness.

Acknowledgements:

The synthesis presented here is that of the author; however, the roots of the referenced traditions originate from ancestors and teachers including, but not limited to: Francesca Mason Boring, Joanna Macy, Bert Hellinger, Shakyamuni Buddha, and countless Dharma teachers.

References:

Macy, J. and M. Brown. 2014 Coming Back to Life: The Updated Guide to The Work That Reconnects. 343 pgs. New Society Publishers. Gabriola Island, BC. Canada.

Mason Boring, F. and K. E. Sloan. Eds. 2013 Returning to Membership in Earth Community: Systemic Constellations with Nature. 195 pgs. Stream of Experience Productions, Pagosa Springs, CO, USA.

Bio:

Matthew Ramsay (he/him), M.Sc., P.Ag., RTC., is a Registered Therapeutic Counsellor with the Association of Cooperative Counselling Therapists of Canada, Certified NVC Trainer with the Center for Nonviolent Communication, Systemic Constellations Facilitator having trained in the tradition established by Bert Hellinger, facilitator of The Work That Reconnects having trained with Joanna Macy and others, Lay Ordained Soto Zen Buddhist practitioner, and Restoration Ecologist in private practice as an ecological consultant, therapist and facilitator based in the unceded traditional territory of the Coast Salish people also known as British Columbia, Canada. Inquiries can be directed to Compassionate Resolutions Counselling and Education, available here:

https://www.compassionateresolutions.ca/

Nature and Me- We Humans Destroy the Environment: What is my part? A Meditation with Bertold Ulsamer

Nature & I, humans destroy nature what is my role? What is your roll.

I invite you to come into this meditation with me and to find more clarity about yourself

If you are ready close your eyes and breathe, notice your breath and with each outbreath you relax a little bit more. You feel the weight of your body and give it to the ground, to the earth.

Now, I invite you to see one place before you. And, this is the place where you see and experience nature in your daily life and in your weeks and weekends, so nature, maybe at home, you have flowers at home, you have a garden. This is nature, and you remember and you see that nature around you, beautiful. And you enjoy it often.

You feel yourself and you breathe.

And, then there is another place around you and this is the place where you know in the news and internet or even in your life how humans destroy nature, and you can see some of these images. Your knowledge is coming up. Pollution of the air, less animals, species die, so you know that and in this place you come in contact with this knowledge, and you feel yourself and you breathe.

And then leave this place also, and there is one place more, and this is all that you know of the magnitude of nature: there are tsunamis, there are earthquakes, floods, fires. So. You know and see that there is something overwhelming, it's big and enormous. And you breathe.

And you feel yourself facing that.

And then the last place, nature, this is you too. You are a child of nature, an animal in some way, so just feel yourself right now, feel the nature in you, the aliveness.

And breathe.

And feel yourself.

And you will walk through all of these four places two times more and each time it deepens. Something becomes more clear for you.

So, if you are ready, we go to the first place. The nature around you in your daily life. Just see what you can see what is arising for you in your inner eye. Animals, flowers, trees, landscapes, the sun, the rain, this is nature around you. And, you accept it, you take it in, and you breath, and you feel yourself, facing nature at this place.

And then you go to the second place again. This is pollution, this is death, how human beings destroy rivers, destroy rivers, destroy animals, and you know that, and you face it right now. And you feel what is going on in you, maybe fear, maybe panic, whatever,

And you breathe

And then you go to the third place. Nature in its essence with the violence of it, the power, you know that thunderstorms are coming, you may become afraid, and the earthquakes again, and volcanoes, bursting out of the fire of the earth. You know that there is life and death in nature. So there are animals who eat other animals. They need to catch them. So, you see that. There's a coming and going, arising and falling. This is nature too.

And you breathe, and you feel yourself.

Allow any emotion that is coming up. Maybe it is the child in you, or the ancestor who was really afraid of nature. These tribes in the jungle, nobody had shelter, this feeling of animals, this is all in our genes.

And you breathe.

Then you go to the fourth place. You as a natural being, your blood, your bones, your breath, this is all nature. And you feel yourself.

And then the last turn

You start with the first place. This is nature in your daily life. Probably soft nature, or very often soft. Beautiful, you enjoy it. Flowers are a gift. Dogs and cats are so nice to human beings. So, whatever is coming up just receive it, this nature around you.

And you feel yourself and you breathe.

And then you go to the next place, human beings who destroy nature. And you are also part of that. You know what you are doing. The car that you are driving. The airplane you are catching and taking. You know how you pollute the atmosphere. If you would not be there, there would be a little less damage So you are here and you damage nature. And you see that. You see you are part of the whole. You are greedy too when you buy cheap clothes and you know it causes damage in the nature and the environment. But this greed once in a while is stronger so just face yourself as a part of the humans who destroy nature.

And breathe.

This is you too.

And then go to the third place. And again there is this overwhelming nature. Much bigger than any human beings, which has its own laws. There is this becoming and rising And, then there's leaving and death. This abundance in nature. One little bird tries to catch the worms for his nest for the young birds, or thousands and thousands, hundreds of thousands of eggs of some fishes and only a few survive. Such abundance, and we are part of that, like ants. So human beings are natural world and they are all over the world, like termites in a way. We build and we grow.

This is also nature. So whatever is coming up, just receive it.

And then go to the last place. This is you. You are nature. You are alive.

This nature of you. The body. The mind is also part of nature, you brain. You can feel your body right now while you are sitting. You can feel the breath and the blood and the heartbeat. This is nature.

And then, just find a center. You have walked the four places, now find the center, or a place where you can see all the four places, observe them, perceive them. This is a place beyond, and you know all of that.

And I have a sentence which sometimes helps to relax:

I don't need to understand.

And you tell yourself this sentence. And you know this all is much bigger and you are a part of all of that. Your body, your life, is a part of this bigger life and this life guides you and leads you.

So just feel the trust in yourself. There is this life which is much bigger which is leading you, your little mind, your little brain, just feel that you can surrender to the bigger life force. And, if not, it's also fine, it's also part of the life in you.

Just breathe

And we can still have a little bit of silence You allow whatever is coming up. And you allow to dive even deeper. And then, slowly, slowly, in your own rhythm come back. So, you move a little bit the body, your shoulders the neck and you open your eyes.

Welcome back and feel the trust in yourself. The trust in life. And out of this life, out of this trust, the good actions will come in your life.

Bio: Bertold Ulsamer, is a first-generation facilitator of family constellation, author of more than twenty books on constellation work, communication, self-management and personal development, Bertold holds a PhD in law, is a certified clinical psychologist, NLP trainer, trauma therapist (Peter Levine) and a respected international teacher.

www.ulsamer.com

Meditations: Belonging Within in the System of Nature

The following are two meditations which were included in a course on Nature Constellations produced by the Real Academy (2020). These may serve as a personal meditation; they may be used as an opening or closing for a group which is exploring Nature Constellations or including Nature as a resource for any system. These meditations may also simply be an introduction which stimulates one's on exploration of bringing Nature, and our systemic relationship to the environment into meditation.

Meditation I: My family and nature: trans-generational gratitude and honoring

Welcome to this module of Nature Constellation. In this time of increased understanding of our relationship to nature and Nature's relationship with us, it is good to make a place, have a time, to fully expand, to make space for the trans-generational relationships of our families to nature. The land, the animals, the air, the water, the landscape, the bounty.

Take a moment to orient yourself. Your heart has brought you to a place where you have a wish to be able to learn, and serve through Nature Constellations.

As we take this journey trust your body and your inner knowing to recognize what feels right for you. Nothing is mandatory. You are welcome to participate, and you are also welcome to simply find your own way of centering, relaxing and connecting with those aspects of nature that are comfortable for you.

Take a relaxing breath.

Find the place in which you are most comfortable. Sitting, lying down, leaning back, whatever feels comfortable to your body, feel into that for a moment. Feel free to close your eyes, or keep your eyes open if you prefer. Whatever feels most relaxed and whatever most supports your inner journey.

We will just breathe for a moment while you find that place.

Breathing in, focus on what you need. What do you need to let go? What do you need to feel at ease? Both in your body and in your soul. Find that place.

Without effort, allow awareness to come to you. As you find stillness, gradually become aware of the longstanding relationship your family has had with nature and that nature has had with your family.

Allow the perception of your soul to recognize and acknowledge what the land has given to your family.

Without effort, become aware of the shelters the earth has provided. No need to judge, or think...just simply allow those images, those dwellings to come to you. Some may be warm caves, or homes made of wood or stone. You may become aware of homes made of animal skins, or walls covered with furs to provide warmth. Just breathe and allow yourself to notice.

There is nothing to debate, this is not a test, it is just a noticing, a recognizing and remembering the earliest relationship that your family had with nature. Perhaps you feel to allow yourself to warm by a fire that is being fueled with wood, or peat, or some kind of animal dung. No need to analyze, simple feel and relax into your remembering journey. You may become so relaxed in this remembering that if we were to stay you would find a warm place and lie down. Take a moment to experience that deep relaxation. Journeying on, take in all that benefits you in this experience, and allow yourself to be energized by the vision and for a moment pause. Noticing that you are looking back in time, these are the aspects of nature that cared for your family, earth, stone, wood, animal.

In your awareness, breathe in the generosity of these care-givers and simply say:

Thank you.

Meditation II: I Am Part of the System of Nature.

So now, simply begin to breathe. Begin to feel and hear your own heart-beat, feel your own body as it expands gently with each breath, and purposefully exhales. As we breathe in, we are accepting the gift of the plants. Gently, allow your body to accept the gift of oxygen. Take your time.

Breathing, relaxing your body. Listening and feeling all that is around you that serves. Life can be busy, but this is a moment in which you can pause and give yourself the space to be cared for and nourished by nature.

Notice that as you quietly exhale you are reciprocating, responding to the gift of oxygen that the plants and trees and grasses have provided. As you calmly inhale and exhale notice that your outbreath is your body's thank you for the generosity of the growing plants, expelling carbon dioxide.

For a moment as you breathe in and exhale, be aware of the exchange. Notice the plants in close proximity who are caring for you, and aware of your reciprocity. Feel your heart open, not just your lungs and your bloodstream, but notice the ability you have to take the gift of nature into your heart. Notice that you are in perfect rhythm with the plants around you. Notice that they are in perfect rhythm with you. There is nothing to push, just notice.

Take your time. As you begin to envision and embody the flow connecting you and all that is growing in nature, notice that you are actually, in a delicate way, united. You are one in your generosity, your purpose is aligned, your respiration is in harmony, you are together. As you become aware of this benevolent ancient agreement, you are joined. You and the plant life are nature, together.

Relaxing into this awareness, you may feel the sense of the antiquity of this rhythm. Without effort, just be aware of the many generations …the two legged and the plant people who have been in relationship for centuries. Calmly breathing, just notice. And it may be that you are aware of a thank you. Perhaps your own, perhaps the echo of many generations, an honoring of the ability to have kept each other alive through the ages.

Gently breathing be aware of the rhythm and the movement of the air coming into your body, going back into the air. Notice that there is no interruption between the air and your breath. The particles outside of your body combine with the breath that you share. You are actually one with the air. You and the air, the wind, are extensions of each other. Uninterrupted. As you quietly breath in a relaxed way you become aware that you are also one with all who have ever breathed. All of your ancestors, all of human kind have breathed the same air. The trees and plants have processed this air for thousands of years.

Enjoying the stillness and the calm, become aware of the saliva in your mouth. The water that your body is using for your well-being. Become aware of the water in your body. Give yourself the time to say thank you to the water in your body. The water in your muscles: thank you...the water in your heart: thank you, the water in your brain: thank you, the water in your kidneys: thank you, the water in your lungs: thank you. For a moment allow your memory to visit the water in nature. The water in the ocean, rivers, creeks, lakes, rainfall, morning dew. Just take a moment to be with the water in your body and the water that you remember in nature.

(Take your time)

For a moment, honor the water in your body, and the presence of water in nature.

Perhaps you can say to the Universe, God, Nature: Thank you for the water.

Your breath, the air, the water... all plant life, the ancestors, each is entwined in an ancient ritual, a natural honoring each other's presence. It is natural, breathing in and comfortably exhaling, be aware that you interwoven with nature. It is completely natural.

Take a breath, relax, perhaps you may feel to say in your heart, or aloud: I am one with nature. This is my nature. I am not alone.

Sitting with the Stories of Brokenness
By Stuart Taylor

the story of no story
the story of no heritage
the story of disconnect and borrowed mythology
the possibility of a potent quest
if you asked your own personal dreaming
what story would you wake with in the morning?
what are the stories of wanderer's
not rooted to a landscape?
are they stories of exile
because we need to return in some way?
not to a landscape
but to an ecosystem
tales are definitely wanderers and shapeshifters
the edge of the known
where so many interesting things happen
what happens at the edge of the village
to masculinities and femininities - vistas open up
a murmuration of souls
an invitation to becoming and to being different

masculine and feminine spirits
flowing freely through us all again
like the spirits present in the wild forests
that remain in the forests that remain
that remain in the forests that remain
let's embrace the alchemy of our senses
nature always offers the perfect medicine
let us have the courage to reawaken our wildness
the wildness inside us so we can feel again
feel the keenness of life the shimmering
energy of the sensuousness that pulses
within us and between us
let's cross-pollinate our prayers
together dream into ancient-future spaces
standing poised at the edges of emergence
emotional intelligence comes to the fore
as a man i dress for the sun and the moon
as a woman i dress for the sun and the moon
i bow to grace 24 / 7 / 365
let's become something more fluid and free
broadening the energies we consider
in our humanness
our energies of animality energies of spirit-being
our new job in the masculine
integrate these inner vulnerabilities
whilst remaining connected to our outer strengths
a dance of integration moving past duality
in the dark forest danger is present
not evil in a human sense but wild
we are tested in its thickets
modernity is deathly afraid of it
the connection between beauty and terror

yes it is profound
modernity and its dreadful spawn colonialism
is where the evil resides not the wilds of the forest
where the spirits run free
let's listen for the voices of our ancestors
their blessing a true treasure
the anthropocene our worst creation
the hypermasculinity of our times
the forest always knows where we are
each one's entry point and threshold
will look and be different
it's all story no matter where we're coming from
in the realm of story we can find treasures
an understanding that we humans are not exceptional
we are not the centre it's not all about us
let's cross-pollinate our prayers
together dream into ancient-future spaces
standing poised at the edges of emergence
emotional intelligence comes to the fore
as a man i dress for the sun and the moon
as a woman i dress for the sun and the moon

Bio: Stuart Taylor is an Artist, Organisational Development Consultant, Systemic Constellator & published Writer. He is London based and has over thirty years international experience working across activist, charity, corporate, education, social justice & therapeutic environments. taylorman1963@gmail.com

Bees In Constellations

In the Seattle, Washington years ago, I facilitated a Nature Constellation (as vision quest). There, a number of people stood representing various aspects of nature and followed the movement, noticing the teaching of who they represented, gradually becoming a part of the natural system that created itself through movement. Following the movement, multiple representatives found that they were compelled through movement to create little micro-systems...the duck representative felt pulled to stand by the representative for the pond, and the dragon fly representative felt drawn to them-even though in larger constellations people cannot possibly remember in a conscious way who is representing what.

In the constellation:

One representative felt invited to represent a particular bush in the area.

Another representative felt invited to represent a bee.

As a facilitator I became nervous because no one felt drawn to represent a flower. I asked the bee representative..."Do you need a flower?"

The representative for the bee said, "No, I am very strong when I stand by this bush."

When we closed the constellation, I shared that we do not always understand everything in a Nature Constellation. I shared that I did not understand why the bee did not need a flower and felt so secure beside the particular bush.

Of course- it just happened that someone in the circle was a biologist with a specialty in botany. He said he was astounded and absolutely understood. He explained to us that the bush was native to the area and was quickly disappearing. You cannot find the bush at any commercial plant nursery because it is considered unattractive. Further, most landscapers remove the bush if it is standing on a construction development site. So, as a 'weed-tree' this bush is becoming more and more rare in the area.

What he further explained was that this particular bush has the highest protein content of any plant in the area, so in the spring when the bees are beginning to come to life in this cold area, they can quickly find the most efficient fuel through this bush. The constellation showed that the bee needs this bush.

***

It has been my privilege to facilitate a number of constellations for bee keepers (apiarists). In one instance the constellation was to identify the location for the bees which would be most conducive to their wellbeing. The space in the circle represented the grid of the property, with North, South, East and West designated. It was possible to have representatives walk through the grid and describe their sensations, level of comfort or discomfort as they felt into the length and breadth of the space. The information was salient for the client.

Constellations have been done to investigate farming of domestic vs. wild bees. Again, with an openness to having clarification regarding what would serve the bees.

In one constellation, when bees were placed in proximity to the individual who cared for the bees, the primary revelation which reverberated with many who were involved in the constellation was the intensity of the benevolence, even love, that the bees had toward the human being who cared for them. What emerged was a visceral understanding that the bees were a resource for the person. Their appreciation, connection, presence, and relationship with the beekeeper was palpable.

This connection, bee to bee keeper, was something that in earlier times was a given. In many traditions there was a consensus that the bees would leave the hive, or die, if they were not allowed to mourn the death of the one with whom they had a bond.

Of interest is that the tradition is relegated to 'superstition' in most of the accounts. In Nature Constellation this deep connection of the bees to their human is confirmed. In reading how prevalent and respected this need to include the bees in the grieving process was (in just one area of the world) the dismissal or ignorance of this connection in modernity is rather glaring.

It feels important to include some of the beliefs and customs in European circles. It is clear that what are generally considered indigenous cultures have long lived with a paradigm which included deep relationship with elements of nature. This brief summary gives some indication that what has been excluded for the sake of 'rational thinking' goes beyond the sphere of what we are aware of in contemporary tribal societies. In the following, it is clear that even in European communities there were pockets of community who were in conversation, in relationship, with the bees.

In The Honey Makers, (Morley, 1899) there is an account of the tradition of 'telling the bees' of the death of their bee-keeper. Published under public domain there is value in sharing and considering something of this understanding.

In earlier times throughout parts of Europe bees were told of the death of their keeper. There were tales of bees dying if this tradition was not observed. Folks in the mountains of North Carolina, USA also practiced some inclusion of the bees when their keeper passed.

In some instances the bee hives were adorned in some way to signify the mourning of the bees.

In addition to describing a life connection between the bees and human caretakers, there are throughout the texts of the 1800's accounts of bee keeping, places which document the conflict between the more modern heirs of deceased bee-keepers and the traditions of including the bees in the bereavement rituals for those who had cared for the bees. This ignoring the grief of the bees often reportedly resulted in the death of the bees, or distress in the hives.

Some traditions involve knocking gently on the hives and announcing that the bee-keeper has died. Some rituals involve burying a piece of the beekeeper's clothing close to the hives.

In some locations, bees were actually taken to the funeral.

In Nature Constellations we have opportunity once again to be in relationship with these winged six-legged beings, and many others who have been waiting for our appreciation, inclusion and respect.

Chris and the Bumblebee
By Chris Walsh, MBBS, DPM, FAChAM

When we turn around to face our traumas without mind numbing substances, we can easily become deadly serious. We can lose touch with playfulness.

This message was communicated to me in a very powerful and mildly embarrassing experience that I had in a workshop run by a Native American woman, Francesca Mason Boring. This experience falls into the category of bizarre and unexplainable. It is a sort of experience that airy fairy new age types go to town on. Even though I have serious concerns about that, the experience was so sweet and illustrative that I want to share it here. For a moment, I will allow the playful energy of this experience to dance across these pages.

This workshop was held on a beautiful sunny spring day near Lake Bernreid in Bavaria in the South of Germany. We were invited to quietly wander around the colourful fragrant gardens of the convent in which we were staying. As we did that, we were supposed to notice if there is any particular part of nature that we were making a special connection with. It could be a tree, a flower, a stream, a bird, an animal or an insect for example.

As I wandered around this beautiful garden, a stupid bumblebee kept inelegantly flying across my path with its uncoordinated, irregular, staccato movements. This was not what I was looking for so I ignored it. I was looking for something serene, something with gravitas. The bumblebee had no gravitas whatsoever! But it was a persistent little bug. It would just keep turning up as I wandered around the garden. Quite impolitely, I told it to piss off. But to no avail. Eventually I surrendered. Clearly, I was not going to connect with something dignified and serene. On that particular day, this crazy little bumblebee was my connection, like it or not.

Francesca then asked us all to form into subgroups of three. We were told to keep our experiences walking in the garden to ourselves. But we are asked to place the other two people in the group to represent our experience. One was to represent ourselves and the other was to represent the element of nature we connected with.

The participants in this workshop were all people who were very familiar with the process called family constellations. This meant that they trusted impulses that came up when they were representing. And this is where it gets really crazy! Remember the representatives of the aspect of nature that we had connected with, had no idea what exactly they were representing.

The person representing the bumblebee started flapping her arms. She said I am flying but I'm not a bird. The person representing me was turning the other way away from the representative of the bumblebee. The bumblebee rep kept dancing and jumping around flapping her arms as she kept trying to get in the face of my representative. My representative finally succumbed to the bumblebee's crazy charms and started smiling at the bumblebee rep. They then were happily interacting. Much to my amazement, these two representatives had played out my whole experience.

I might have guessed that they had been spying on me, it was so accurate. However, I knew they were not, as when I was wandering through the garden, I had noticed them in the distance deeply involved in their own experience connecting to nature, whatever that was.

As I observed these two representatives replay my experience I started to laugh and really get in touch with the bumblebee playfulness.

After each of the three people in the little groups had been through this process with their own experience, we all returned to a room on the second floor of the conference centre. Much to everyone's merriment, when I related my story, a bumblebee flew in through the window and started its crazy bumble dancing right in front of the group leader, Francesca Mason Boring.

This experience was something I desperately needed at the time. This while I was writing this book several years later, Francesca sent me an email asking if she could share this story in a book she was writing. I was very happy for her to do so and that the same time I was writing this chapter and realised it would be very apt here as well.

This email revitalised my inner bumblebee right at the moment that I was getting heavily into this deadly serious narrative about trauma. It was perfect. The bumblebee again gave me a sense of lightness that I desperately needed. Regardless of how traumatised we might be, we all need this in our playful interactions with family and friends, with nature and with the arts. That is also an important part of healing and enjoying life. Traumatised indigenous communities, survivors of the Holocaust and any other traumatised groups do well to remember and revitalise their traditional songs, dance and ceremonies. We are doing well if we can remember how to laugh. There is no shame in allowing ourselves to be undignified silly bumblebees from time to time.

Bio: Dr. Chris Walsh MBBS DPM FAChAM. is a bilingual psychiatrist working in private practice in Melbourne. His psychotherapy integrates diverse theoretical frameworks. including Mindfulness, CBT. Gestalt and Self Psychology. He has worked in jails. community settings. and drug and alcohol institutions as well as with urban and tribal Aboriginal communities and with the military.

Chris Walsh has received mindfulness teacher training, as well as some relevant spiritual transmissions. He has been practicing this form of meditation for over twenty-five years. Chris has organically integrated Mindfulness Meditation into his psychiatric practice from the beginning of his training as a result of assisting at the Tibetan refugee hospital in Dharamsala in Northern India when in 1983. He has been actively teaching it for over 25 years.

Chris has taken a major role in Constellation Work in Australia. He organized the first Australasian Intensive which was uniquely successful. He was on the training faculty there and at the North American Intensive training. He has given presentations at Australian national and international professional conferences on both Mindfulness and Family Constellations and had articles published on both topics. Chris founded and moderated the international email group Constellation Talk from 2003 to 2020.

Seeds:

The people who live here now don't talk to me the way the people who used to live here."

Two different representatives for Nature in two different constellations spoke these same words a few weeks apart, in two different locations in two different circles. The only two things these groups had in common were me, the facilitator, and the voice of Nature. That caught my attention. When Nature speaks in her own voice, it always catches my attention. It's always a revelation.

The first constellation which brought forth these words was an impromptu one. I asked if anyone would be willing to do a small constellation to explore the dynamics of a recent Andean style offering I'd given to a local spring on our mountain. Something hadn't gone quite right in that offering, and I wanted to find out more about what that was. Could someone be the Rocks? Could someone be the Trees? Could someone be the Spring? Sure, they said. And so we began.

When the representatives found their places and settled, the Field held a pregnant fullness. It is the fullness I sense when the Field is ready to speak. When I checked in, I didn't't get much. Perhaps something was missing? I asked a pillow and some small objects to represent the offering I had made. I placed the offering in front of the Spring as I had done at the spring itself. "That's nice" said the Spring in a flat, neutral way. I added some minor objects to represent each item I'd put into the offering.

I asked the Spring, "is this better?" She replied, "it's ok." I had in my body the echo of my physical offering still not being fully received. I had felt this when I made my offering on the mountain a few days before. I was puzzled. Something was missing. And that's when she said: "The people who live here now don't talk to me the way the people who used to live here." Humbled, I asked: "What would you have me do differently?" "You didn't't touch me" said The Spring. "You need to touch me." As I touched the Spring-rep's knee gently, she sighed and closed her eyes in bliss. The other representatives smiled, relaxed, and began to move together. We all felt bigger and stronger as the message flowed into each of us.

What I have learned from this and countless other Nature Constellations is to listen, to let go of what I think I know, to completely let go of my limited human ideas about how I think Nature organizes herself. Only then will she trust me with her truth, with the actual what-is. When that pregnant fullness arrives in the Field of a Nature Constellation, I know that that I have gained her trust. And my own.

Jeffrey Rich facilitates Nature Constellations and Systemic Constellations in an Animist tradition

jeffrey.rich@gmail.com

LivingEnergy.Life

NATURE CONSTELLATIONS
By Amdal-Rafael Ruiz

One of the most fascinating endeavors, for me, in systemic constellation work has been learning about Nature Constellations. Using constellations in order to experience and solve problems related to nature has been very valuable, since fundamentally it allows us to reconnect with our Great Mother. Life of this planet has been propitiated, sustained and nurtured by Nature and is not separate from it. Her forceful voice has a silent quality that humans may not always recognize and much less interpret, with fatal consequences that now everyone can recognize. Nature Constellation work allows us to come close to Nature's voice in several ways and through many different elements that may manifest themselves when represented.

Although Constellation work is surely not the only means for us to contact with Nature, it has evolved, as a profound, simple way, of relating to her, and to listen to her voice. Shamans, Yogis, Mystics, Meditators from many cultures and traditions have been channeling and speaking from and for Nature. Many are also contributing now to the evolution of constellation work.

Within my limited experience in Nature Constellations I have been fortunate enough to facilitate them in the several contexts and forms, according to the demands from family constellation workshops as well as ecological issues that concern the groups I've worked with. Some of the experiences have evolved while working with students training in Facilitating Constellations.

Nature Constellations can be done indoors, when there is an issue in a family constellation that involves nature, gardens, land, ecological problems, animals, etc. These themes can also be facilitated locating the constellation in nature itself, which opens up other possibilities for The Knowing Field can manifest phenomenon that nature shows directly, like wind, rain, and appearance of animals, that add significance to the constellation. A third and distinct modality happens when in other forms of constellations, family constellation or other systemic constellations, we want to introduce elements of nature so that it may add wisdom and strength to a particular situation.

Nature Constellations Indoors:

On several occasions we have had the opportunity, during a family constellation workshop, for configuring a constellation with problems felt by the group that had to do with land, gardens, plagues, pets, and other concerns. A piece of land that had difficulties for its commercialization often showed species whose needs had to be taken into account, and when that happened, things began to flow again for the persons involved. When animals or plants can express themselves, they clearly manifest their needs and, since they are always interrelated with other factors, like commercialization, housing or productivity, when their needs are taken into account, new possibilities open up.

Specific Nature Constellations done indoors can have a theme related to nature, like an ecological problem. These constellations in Queretaro, Mexico have had various themes related to concerns that have been expressed by various groups and that have to do specifically with our community: shortages of water resources, Park Cimatario, a natural reserve that has been taken by developers; and the disappearance of species in the surroundings, both fauna and flora, like, deer, *cacomixtle* (a native rodent of raccoon family), several species of cactus and others.

In order to choose the theme we usually ask an open question to the group. One group expressed interest on working on the **effect of urbanization on water shortage** in Queretaro which was a common concern. The following roles for representation came up: Water, the Land, Ancestors, Present population and New population, Government, Developers.

An interesting event in this constellation was the fact that the population was divided, half on one side and half on the other. The Representative for Water was moving everywhere, interacting with the other Representatives, as if flowing all over the place. In this constellation the Land (nature) did not seem to be concerned and remained in the center, while other representatives gathered around her. The Representatives for the Developers and the Representatives for The Present Population were able to express their needs for housing and urbanization. At first it seemed to have conflict with the land but eventually both came together. The water's role was very impressive for in flowed with everyone and finally became a unifying factor.

In another constellation with the theme of **Land abuse**, there were representatives for Mother Earth, Corporations, Humanity, Government and Money. At the beginning Corporations and Government started making secret arrangements between them, cooperating for land exploitation and Humanity was indifferent and everyone turned to look at Money and nobody looked at Mother Earth. She reported feeling pain. Also initially there was enmity between Humanity and the Government but eventually they felt they had the same interests and turned to look at Mother Earth, although they did not get close to her. Corporations stayed away, apparently angry at these movements. Eventually the resolution came when everyone was able to look at Mother Earth.

One more constellation was facilitated, in which the concern for water took a slightly different aspect, related to the **aquifer mantles in Queretaro.** On this occasion the representative included: Water, Aquifer Mantles, Earth, Present Population, Authorities, Economic interests, Futures Population and later Greater Hands appeared. What was very clear in this constellation was that Water felt itself always crystalline and going through ravines and fields. Everyone seemed to move within their own agendas and at first there was little interaction. Finally someone came in to represent Greater Hands. This person set up a chair in the middle and stepped on top of it. All the other representatives were then moved towards her and there seemed to be some equilibrium. The Authorities at first were drawn to the Economic interests, then to the Population. Even the Economic interests who had wandered around trying to find a place and feeling rejected by all, finally found their place there with Greater Hands. The Representative of the Authorities brought together the Representative for Economic Interests, Future Population and the Land. Water walked around surrounding all of them.

Another constellation had the theme of **Disappearance of deer in the Reserve by Mt. Cimatario in Queretaro,** we chose to represent: Deer, The Land of the park, Water, Squirrels, Government, Population, Water.

What was expressed, beyond the search for conflict between the representatives was the lack of aquifers in the land. The Deer were migrating away from the land, following the Representative for Water.

Animal Constellations:

One of my first experiences with Animal Constellations came during a Family Constellation Workshop in which a person, now living alone, was concerned about the wellbeing of several dogs and cats that lived with her. She told me the theme ahead of time trying to be sure it would be appropriate. Since at the time I was reluctant to ask persons to represent animas, I suggested we do a blind constellation.

It was an amazing constellation for the Representative of the woman sat down in the middle of the floor and all the other representatives, who didn't know they represented dogs and cats, came towards her and lied down by her. After a while this representative reported being overwhelmed and decided to stand up. The representatives of the animals said they were content with this move and felt more secure this way. She understood that her animals expected her to be more assertive with them and assume her alpha place within them.

On another occasion, a training group had the need to feel the representation of animals and one woman was feeling sad about the death of one of her dogs. She was a person that had adopted several dogs (6), cats (2), about 4 turtles, as well as several parrots. She wanted to know how the animals interacted on her absence and with the death of the dog. This time the representatives did not know which animal each represented. The dead dog, named Chi, had blessed its owner's absence. Several parrots were represented as well as turtles, dogs and cats. When the owner was able to say good by to the dead dog every other animal felt better and they said that they accompanied her. The animals complained that when she went away the man that helped take care of them did was not attending their needs, they reported that they had suffered for being thirsty. When we put a representative for the man, he acknowledged that he was not happy doing this job. The animals expressed discontent with him and said they liked the previous carer. This one needed better organization but mostly lacked caring. But they said they preferred to stay at home and not be taken to another place. One of the dogs said he was lonely because he lacked a partner. When we put a representative for the parter, then he was very happy.

In a constellation where trees has grown too big and were affecting the foundations of the house. The house thank them for their shade and protection and the trees said they gave permission for trimming and would appreciate being trimmed and not cut altogether. In the days that followed, there was a trimming done by the municipality of the city.

In another constellation when there was a plague of ants in a garden. The ants said they were harmless and that there was much work to do. They needed to be thanked. Although in this case the ants continued to come, somehow they became less of a plague and their work was incorporated into the appreciation of the landscape.

Family Constellations in Nature:

Within time we have done several constellations "in nature" in different cites around Queretaro.

In San Joaquin, a small town in the mountains of Sierra Gorda, where there are ancient Pre Colombian ruins, a place of rainforest with big Pine Trees that had been reforested. There we worked with **Family Constellations in Nature**.

The theme of one family constellation had to do with a partner that had gone away. Representatives were a mixture of nature and personal characters, like The Seeker, Her Partner. the Ancestors, Land, Trees, Leaves and Animals of the woods. The Representative for the leaves on the ground spoke of dead and regeneration as the carpet of dead leaves lay under us. There had been someone dead, apparently an abortion. The woman concerned mourned on the ground, where among rich earth full of leaves, many small spiders had spread thin webs. These disturbed her so she was forced to get up. Although she had pain for her loss, she realized that there was more life around her. The indifference of nature, leaves and trees, seemed to give her a comforting sense and she understood that not having been able to process the loss of the child with her partner had to do with their separation.

Several other constellations had as their scenery a Ranch not far from the town of Amealco, also in Querétaro. In this region there are also some small forests with high altitude flora. The weather is usually fresh. This place, by the name of **Rancho Calixto,** is located a few miles outside the city near a rural community, that is rapidly growing, called Chiteje de la Cruz. Its owner, a young man that inherited several acres of land, has built wooden cabins and offers the place for small retreats and leisure. He has been caring for the forest, recreating several species of animals that slowly are returning, like deer, squirrels, several species of rabbits, different kinds of birds and even ajotoles (a native type of fish that is in danger of extintion). Besides caring for the forest, he has ventured in agriculture, building several green houses. With this combination of natural tourist, restoration of the forest and agricultura, he had been trying to make ends meet. He is also reproducing several species of quail and has chickens. He had been attempting to develop this areas in order for the ranch to survive, but had several difficulties: besides economic, authorities were slow at granting him permits and there were other interests in the community, as well as corrupt authorities in the municipality.

Our training group chose this place in order to spend a weekend specially dedicated to learning Nature Constellations. There is a main Hall where they prepare meals, and since it has a large area for dinning, it could be used for our gatherings in a capacity of around 40 persons.

In this place we did four constellations, two about nature, in the woods and another inside the big hall. And two more relating to animals, one for animals in the forest and another for a woman that was having difficulties with her pets.

The forest area must be about 40 acres in all. Before entering a woman in the group led a native ritual from the ancient dwellers, where we honored the land and asked permission to work there and learn from it.

This constellation in the forest consulted about the regeneration of the forest. Representative were picked for Birds, Eagles, Owls, Cacomixtle (a rodent similar to a Raccoon), Deer and Black Salamander, that often migrates there's and Ajolote (a type of native fish that is in danger of extinction) The Forest and the Trees were also represented. Later, Squirrels were also introduced protesting that they had not been taken into consideration. In general the Animals felt well for returning to the forest, saying they had enough to eat. Deer complained that they needed more water and that they felt the owner was not attending them well enough. There was a general feeling that there was a need for more water in the small dam. The Tree was weeping for deforestation in the region. The Ajolote felt confused and remained close to the Deer. The Green House felt prosperous and saw itself growing. The Rep for Tomato was close to the Green house and felt happy.

A second constellation, in this place, happened inside the main hall. The theme was about **difficulties in sustaining the property.** The Representatives were: The Owner, The Ranch itself, The Green House, The Federal Conservation Agency, Municipal authorities, The Community, The Land.

What the Field showed was a difficulty in communication between authorities and the Owner. The Municipal authorities pulled the Ranch towards them as if they were interested in doing something else with it. Finally the Rep. for The Owner was aided by the Federal Authorities who had been detached from everything. There also seemed to be a conflict between the Community and the Ranch. Part of the solution was the alliance with the Community. Authorities were reluctant to act feeling this conflict. At first the Community was hesitant and a bit jealous about The Owner's project. When The Owner sought their help and honored authorities and with the help of the Federal Rep. finally there was a movement towards a solution.

The Owner finally took his place standing between the Green House and the Ranch feeling optimism. He was deeply moved. We found out that after the constellation the Ranch has gone very well, there is a lot of demand and business keeps flourishing. It is usually busy. RanchoCalixto@RanchoCalixtoAmealco.

Several other constellations in nature happened in a Club Valle Verde, where I reside. One that particular called for our attention was a **Family Constellation in nature.** A man around 40 years old had an issue with his sister. His preoccupation was his sister's relationship to their father. Throughout the constellation the representative for the Sister kept feeling him as intrusive in her relationship with her father. After many movements he did not seem to let the sister go. When we thought that there was no more to be done and he was asked to take his place in the constellation ready to close. However, soon after he took his place, a bird passed by and shit on his head. That was sufficient for him to realize that his argument about the sister's need of him was not real. He felt that his preoccupation was bullshit, a rationalization for not assuming his own needs. His feeling about worrying for her and his feeling burdened were the result of his own overprotective attitudes. He was better as he realized that everyone has to assume its own destiny.

In this place we had also other interesting situations when someone saw twice, and in different places, a Cacomixtle (an animal in Mexico which is similar to a Raccoon). It is a species in danger of extinction and in more than 30 years I have only seen one or two. Driving on his way down there, through a cobble stone road with trees on both sides, he saw this animal that stopped in front of his car for a few moments. At the time he interpreted the animal's behavior to mean that it was saying to him that he should slow down.

Soon after, upon constellating the theme of water shortage that had been expressed, the little animal appeared to him once again. This time representative had been chosen for Aquifer Mantles, Industry, Present and future society, Flora, Fauna and the Ecosystem. During the constellation, at first Industry and Society would not look at Nature and she asked "Why won't they look at me?" Representatives joined and intertwined. The Rep for the Aquifer Mantle said "It is not too late". Here is where the Cacomistle appeared and it was seen by two persons, one of them was the man that had encountered it when he was arriving on the cobble stone road. This time on the constellation it was took to be saying "Continue what you are doing, it is important". After that the Representatives seemed much more integrated.

It seemed that water joined everyone together. What began to unify the system was the Rep. for Water Mantles and Nature.

When the ancestors intervened, there a strong wind and later there was a soft wind at the top of the trees and leaves fell on the participants.

Subsequently, when a constellation about **water reserve** had come to a standstill, the Representative for Ondine's (water Deva) was chased by a bee and it said that we should cease to try and fix things, that water was greater and did not need our intervention. She said "I know how to flow" and she began to sing, at that moment everything started to flow and a soft wind at the top of the trees brought leaves to fall on the circle. With his movements everyone in the constellation started to move again. Human conscience, that was also represented, expressed concern about contamination of the mantles, and it was obvious that humans were doing that. It expressed the suffering of earth because of the good conscience of humans that were contaminating aquifer mantles. That realization made everyone sad and this sadness seemed move everyone and then birds started to sing and dogs barked far away.

In another constellation with this same theme, done outside, there were representatives for Wild, Animals, Earth, People, as well as Water. Water was lying on the ground feeling sad. Everyone turned to see other parts of nature and everyone ended up lying beside and touching the Representative for Water and they felt peaceful.

Family Constellation where elements of nature were represented:

Another important form of Nature Constellation is when we incorporate, in a Family or Systemic Constellation, elements of nature. It seems to me that they give strength and wisdom to a situation. When a seeker in a constellation is facing difficult time and we introduce a representative for some elements of nature, it gives the person the strength to face whatever they may need to confront. Sometimes we may introduce a representative for the land, the country of origin, a house, a tree or any other element that may seem appropriate. But we can also bring the Sun, the moon, the ocean, the wind and always they help. Maybe it has to do with the added consciousness to the seeker, maybe it reminds of greater forces, maybe that help relinquish ego. Whatever we may speculate, what is evident is that it enhances the life forces from within.

Introducing elements from nature in a constellation are most useful when there is an impasse, when the constellation is stagnated or when there are overwhelming negative forces that hinders a process.

PROCEDURES:

It is not my intention to instruct about procedures in Nature Constellations, I simply want to convey what we were doing, taking from the lessons of my teachers but accommodated to the needs of the moment.

1. In constellations that were facilitated indoors but where nature was invited, we followed the regular procedures of Family Constellations, with a Seeker guiding the initial configuration and placing Representatives for nature when it was required, sometimes from the start but others later, and dealt with their input as it was manifested. Needless to say, it always added towards a wiser view of a situation or it gave strength to the Seeker and to the solution of its theme. This same procedure was followed when there was an issue dealing with animals, gardens or land problems for a particular Seeker.

2. When a group that had a concern for an issue related to nature, to ecological problems or any issue related to a common concern, we opened up the question to the circle of participants in order to better define the issue itself and how it was to be named. Once that was defined, sometimes we asked for suggestions about what Representative were needed, sometimes the facilitator named them from intuition and yet others were opened for participants that felt called to fill such representations. At times we put the roles of representation on a piece of paper on the floor, sometimes with the sign down and asked participants to walk through and feel their place there and only at the end, the role was revealed.

3. With Family Constellations in nature we followed standard procedures for them but incorporated, when reading the field's information, all the events that appeared in nature at the moment: wind, rain, shade, animals and tried to make the participants do the same, as well as the Representatives reporting their sensations, feelings and intuitions from their contact with natural elements. Sometimes the field revealed important elements for the constellation. Like when a bumble bee chased a representative or when a bird shit on the Seeker's head of when someone saw an animal appear.

4. In Family and Systemic Constellations, when we need to introduce nature or its elements in order to gain strength or wisdom, we follow the intuition and the clues that the Knowing Field or the seeker may give us. As in other instances, we can always try and see the effects of these representations and regulate the constellation according to these.

SOME LESSONS DERIVED FROM NATURE CONSTELLATIONS:

1. Nature is always moving, it is a dynamic life force that is always regenerating itself and developing. Life flows
2. The movement of life is beyond our wills.
3. Nature is not concerned with its survival, it is beyond it.
4. We are all included. We all belong.
5. There is a natural order and we are all bound by it.
6. Disobeying the natural order is not a sin, it is only being incongruent.
7. The laws of nature follow a movement within the laws of greater possibilities, in more collective systems.
8. Nature in not vengeful; it only follows its greater equilibrium.
9. The equilibrium of nature is always in movement towards more complexity towards higher harmony.
10. There is a harmonic unity in a perfect order.
11. Nature is generous.
12. The laws of nature follow a movement within the laws greater, more collective systems.
13. Diversity in nature is always in harmony, but not without conflict.
14. Nature has no peace it is a dynamic moving system.

We have found that Nature Constellations help us realize that life's movement is beyond our wills. Often we are surprised with the unexpected answers that nature's elements give. Like in the constellation about water shortage, the Rep. for water said "Stop trying to mend things for me, I am greater than you and I don't need your intervention". Our perspective of life and Nature is so narrow; our senses, even our inner senses, have a very limited range compared to most animals. We have mostly lost our intuition, or at least we are so attentive to our rational understandings that we minimize it greatly. Animals and plants, as well as many other elements in nature, are flowing with what happens to them, rather than forcing individual wills on the movements of Nature.

Interest in survival does not seem to be a concern of nature. It seems to be beyond it, living what appears in each present moment. Although this does not mean that there may not be wider movements that carry all and that nature abides by, but these don't seem to be in conflict with each individual being.

The relationship within nature seems to be in perfect harmony. If we accept the cycles of death and rebirth, regeneration is always a transmuting element that appears in nature. Now that mankind is discovering nature's language, in its variations, from chemical to fungi and codes, we can begin to see the fullness of its harmony. Its interaction reveals a coherence that is quite deeper than any human entanglement.

Nature's interaction is so rich that humans are beginning to modify their previous understanding of conflict, tension and decay. The perfect balance that nature shows in a given ecosystem is so delicate and perfect that when discovering it, humanity is not merely amazed, it becomes uplifted. Nature is so much greater than the human species that it has made humanity question whether its forms of consciousness are really such an advantage and an advancement.

Nature is also teaching us that we belong within it, not in the supremacy that our collective Ego had believed. We indeed have a place, and when we accept it, we realize that it is a good place. Even though it may seem that we are the rulers that are putting nature to trial, she is so much more capable, resilient and lasting than humans, she will survive us, and we will continue to belong in whatever comes after.

It is teaching us a natural order, within an incredible diversity of possibilities. When we think about it, we find it amazing that nature has been generous enough to accommodate cities, roads, vehicles, drillings, space stations, radio waves and so many other manipulations that we as humans have been doing. The laws of nature follow a movement with the greater laws within more collective and comprehensive systems. And it has an enormous heart where all fits in.

Nature teaches us that all of our particular orders and patters belong within greater orders, by which we are bound. Disobeying the natural order is not a sin, we are simply being incongruent and must pay the consequences. We are learning that nature is not vengeful, it only follows a greater equilibrium.

The equilibrium of nature is always in movement towards more complexity, towards a higher harmony. There is harmonic unity in perfect order. We as humans are beginning to learn that when we flow with nature's order, one that is included within the Spirit's order, beyond our feeble reasoning, we participate of a higher order and equilibrium. We are bound in a loving way, when we let ourselves follow the Greater Hands that carry it all.

There is a natural generosity that seems to flow in Nature's environments. She simply offers herself. Victims and perpetrators both are nurtured by her and, when given the chance, Nature is bountiful. Even when our particular needs are not met, we still can be a part of that bounty, in the bounty of drought and the bounty of famine when we open our perception and know that we belong in greater clusters, we can begin to experience these also as blessings. Of course not without pain and consequences but we are seeing miracles that make the dessert flourish in lavish colors, that clean a dam or repair an ozone hole.

Nature Constellations have taught us that nature does not give simple answers. She often changes the answer to the same questions especially when they are existential questions. The dynamics of life are revealed regarding each particular situation, within its time and place, its context, always unique and unrepeatable. When we try to make laws and name phenomenon in abstract we are often in a dead end. Only when we are willing to open our perception do we discover a living process in which we cannot separate our knowing from the phenomenon and one that engages us always in a commitment to life, with life.

Often in a constellation, Nature shows itself in its great variety of forms. What is always amazing is the perfect relationship between the parts. They are always in perfect harmony. We cannot find peace in nature if we understand it without conflict. Conflict is part of what moves nature in an always dynamic way. The interaction between different elements of nature is always changing in the sense of transformation. Just as plants transform the sun's energy, soil and water, so do fungi recycle dead material into nutrients, and animals feed on each other. We learn that we, as human beings, are also part of a greater cycle. Maybe then we can stop being frightened by our feeble human destiny.

In Nature Constellations we have a big lesson about diversity and its blessings. There seems to be room for an infinite number of variety of forms, colors, shapes, needs and demands. Yet all have a place in a common harmony where each has its own place and where it receives and gives what it needs, as well as what is necessary for others. We surely are embellished by its colorful variety, but, are we ready to recognize its value for the whole? Diversity is not a whim of those that have felt excluded, nor a vengeful vindication or a concession of the dominant. It is simply a natural way of life. To go against it is denying an imponderable quality of nature's procedures and its essential richness.

One lesson that is hard to listen to is that Nature has no peace. Peace is for the dead, but nature is alive if we begin to understand its movements, its always dynamic change. Regeneration is simply a way for a higher order, for a cycle that moves eternally forward. We want to believe that it is going towards higher more complex forms. Perhaps. Yet our belief is not essential.

It is not clear to me how much of the above reflections came directly from a Knowing Field while we were working with Nature Constellations or whether they are simply thoughts stimulated by the contact with nature in this work. But, whatever it might be I hope they resonate with you as well.

During a Walking Meditation in Nature a participant had a distinct vision of death within nature. She imagined an orchard as a tomb, under whose realization, she began to observe brighter colors and textures as well as olfactory perceptions enhanced. She ceased to be afraid of nature when before the meditation, she had feared coming out in the soft rain that had started to fall. Needless to say, she was not under the influence of any drug. The deep state of meditation gave her the possibility of awareness about a deep truth. Just like my dear loving teacher Thich Nhat Hanh had taught: within being is non-being (paraphrase is mine). Nature always teaches us that in decay is new life, when we can envision greater cycles.

Bio: Amdal Rafael Ruiz is a clinical psychologist from Queretaro Mexico. He graduated from Texas Christian University in 1953 with a B.A. in Psychology and Philosophy. In 1967 Rafael received a M.Div from Union Theological Seminary in New York and later an M.A. in Clinical Psychology at the Universidad Autonoma de Queretaro, where he was a full Professor until 2011. He trained in psychoanalysis, took courses in Gestalt groups, Tanathology, Reiki, and Aromatherapy. In 2003 he trained in Family Constellations with Carola Diduche at the Gestalt Institute in Queretaro and with Bert Hellinger's

Intensive Trainings (7) in Mexico City. Later he also trained with Francesca Mason Boring in Maryland, U.S.A. He has been doing constellation workshops in several cities in Mexico, Guatemala, Honduras, Chile, U.S., Canada and Spain, as well as on line. He has been offering Systemic Constellation trainings in Querétaro and Guatemala since 2011.

Presently he gives private psychotherapy and Training in Constellation work.

amdalihung@gmail.com
amdal11@hotmail.com

Sweet Dreams

This discussion of Nature Constellations, the facilitators, techniques, stories, constellation experiences is just an entry way.

There is so much yet to learn and do in the field of Nature Constellations.

Applying systems constellation to better understand Nature and to take appropriate steps involving environmental issues bodes well for our world. We can begin to encourage taking constellations outdoors, and bringing the outdoors into the constellation when it is indicated.

Constellations have been done to explore converting cash crops from those heavily treated with pesticides to organic products. Organizational and community constellation approaches were a benefit, and it was also helpful to hear from the plants themselves.

Our personal systemic history with place may answer questions about our anxieties and lack of grounding, much like the way in which we found family systems constellation to be so impactful.

Insect infestations that impacted a collective's bottom line as well as 'invaders' have been constellated and we are reminded that we are part of an informational field. We are part of the whole.

We have a viable vehicle to better understand, issues that are impacting all living beings and communities. Nature constellations does not simply give voice to the issues that are challenging us, it literally gives a voice to the components of systemic issues which threaten our biosphere.

One of the most impactful representations I ever stood in was when I represented mycelium. Having a felt sense of the antiquity, the connectivity and the intelligence of this network was impressive. It reminded me of how far we have to go as human beings, and long after the constellation was done it has continued to reminded me that we are held. Under our feet are universes of resilience. Extending our resources and perceptions to include that abundance and effortless interrelatedness can only encourage an unfolding that has hope.

Through nature constellations, we may find solutions, insights, clarity, and in some cases, we quietly, simply, come closer to the Mystery. These possibilities in the hands of many openhearted facilitators and all human beings, helps me relax and breathe more easily.

References

Banyard, I. (2019). The Origin of Forest Bathing, Retrieved 10/21/2021 from https://www.ianbanyard.com/home/the-origin-of-forest-bathing-forest-therapy

Bowen-Gernstein, D. and Williams Christine, (2020). The Surprising Link Between Parks and Violence Prevention, Retrieved 3/1/22 from: https://nextcity.org/urbanist-news/the-surprising-link-between-parks-and-violence-prevention

Burials and Beyond: Life, Death and the Weird Bits in Between, Telling the Bees, Retrieved 2/4/2022 from https://burialsandbeyond.com/2021/04/17/telling-the-bees

Cassella, C. (2020). Daycares in Finland built a 'Forest Floor' and it Changed Children's Immune Systems, Retrieved 1/28/2022 https://www.sciencealert.com/daycares-in-finland-built-a-backyard-forest-and-it-changed-children-s-immune-systems

Chavan, T. (2021). Importance of Nature in Architecture and Design, Retrieved 2/28/2022 from https://www.99acres.com/articles/importance-of-nature-in-architecture-and-designing-2.html

Eglan, G. (2015). Beasts of War: The militarization of animals, Lilu.com

Gosh, A. (2016). The Great Derangement: Climate Change and the Unthinkable, Chicago, University of Chicago Press

Huizen, J. (2019). What to know about eco anxiety Retrieved 10/22/2022 from https://www.medicalnewstoday.com/articles/327354

J Environ Public Health. 2012; 2012: 291541 Retrieved 9/18/2021, from https://www.ncbi.nlm.nih.gov/pmc/articles/PMC3265077

Kim, M. (2016). Retrieved 10/21/2021 from https://www.washingtonpost.com/news/to-your-health/wp/2016/05/17/forest-bathing-is-latest-fitness-trend-to-hit-u-s-where-yoga-was-30-years-ago

Li, Q.(2018). Forest Bathing: How Trees Can Help You Find Health and Happiness, N.Y., N.Y., Viking

Mason-Boring, F. & Sloan, K. (2013). Returning to Membership in Earth Community: Systemic Constellations with Nature, Pagosa Springs, Colorado, Steam of Experience Publications

Mason-Boring, F. (2021) Retrieved 9/18/2021, from https://realacademy.net/courses/nature-constellations

Morley, M. (1899). The Honey-Makers, Chicago, A.C. McClurg and Company

National Forest Foundation, Tree Profile, Aspen: So Much More Than a Tree, Retrieved 6/17/2022 from https://www.nationalforests.org/blog/tree-profile-aspen-so-much-more-than-a-tree

Ritter, L., (2020) The Knowing Field and Field Awareness. Retrieved 6/22/2022 from: https://www.collectivetransitions.com/intro-to-sc-2/the-knowing-field-and-field-awareness

Sanders, L. (2016). Hippocampus makes maps of social space too. Retrieved 3/3/2022 from: https://www.sciencenews.org/article/hippocampus-makes-maps-social-space-too?utm_source=Society+for+Science+Newsletters&utm_campaign=f5c600ab9b-Latest_From_Science_News&utm_medium=email&utm_term=0_a4c415a67f-f5c600ab9b-104661445

Sheldrake, R. (2011). How Dogs Know When their Owners are Coming Home: and other unexplained powers of animals, New York, Three Rivers Press

Stelljes, S. (2018). Bobbie the Wonderdog. Retrieved 2/10/2022 from https://www.oregonencyclopedia.org/articles/bobbie_the_wonder_dog/#.YgVCGd_MKUk

St. Just, A. (2018). Relative Balance in an Unstable World, Create Space Independent Publishing

Tenenbaum, L. (2020). Digging in the Dirt Really Does Make People Happier, Retrieved 9/18/2021 from: https://www.forbes.com/sites/lauratenenbaum/2020/01/29/digging-in-the-dirt-really-does-make-people-happier/?sh=b98081131e1c

Ulsamer, B. (2019). Nature and Me: Humans destroy the environment- What is my Role? Retrieved 9/18/2021 from https://www.youtube.com/watch?v=gWWbSz6mVIQ&t=69s

Wall Kimmerer, R. (2013). Braiding Sweetgrass: Indigenous wisdom, scientific knowledge and the teaching of plants, Minneapolis, MN, Milkweed Editions

Wilson, D. (2019). Grounding: Exploring Earthing Science & the Benefits of It. Retrieved 6/22/2022 from: https://www.healthline.com/health/grounding

About the Author:

Francesca Mason Boring is a bi-cultural author, international facilitator and trainer of Family Constellation. Mason Boring has been a key figure in the development of the integration of ceremony and ritual in constellation work as well as the inclusion of nature in facilitation, as support for personal and trans-generational trauma. Her writing and developments in systemic constellation include applications of the work in social systems as well as family systems. A Western Shoshone, Francesca has authored numerous books and Co-edited the first book on Nature Constellations: Returning to Membership in Earth Community: Systemic Constellations with Nature. In addition she has served as an advisor and contributing writer for The Knowing Field, an international scholarly journal on systems constellation, England and is a member of the International Systemic Constellations Association. Francesca has provided workshops and presented at numerous conferences in Germany, Italy, Switzerland, Singapore, Holland, Mexico, Canada, Australia, South Africa, Bulgaria and the United States. She has served on faculty for

Intensives on Systemic Constellations in Germany, Mexico, Australia, and the U.S.A., and has been providing systems constellation workshops and trainings for facilitators in family and human systems constellations for more than 20 years. www.allmyrelationsconstellations.com

"For me, systems constellation is one of the most profoundly beautiful healing paths that can be taken. This work is an extension of Ceremony, a road of indigenous healing. The ancestors are not just an allegory traditionally; they are an available resource." -Francesca

Additional Publications by Francesca Mason Boring

Family & Systems Constellation: In the Company of Good People (2019)

Family Systems Constellations and Other Systems Constellation Adventures: A transformational journey, (2015) All My Relations Press. Bulgarian translation: (2018) Arts & Therapy Foundation-Bulgaria.

Returning to Membership in Earth Community: Systemic Constellations with Nature, (2013) Edited by Francesca Mason Boring & Kenneth Edwin Sloan, Stream of Experience.

Connecting to our Ancestral Past: Healing through Family Constellation, Ceremony & Ritual, (2012) North Atlantic Books (Distributed by Random House) Previously published as: Notes from_the Indigenous Field: Family & Systems Constellation, Ceremony & Ritual, (2011)Create Space.

Wandelen door het wetende veld: Rituelen en Ceremoniën in Systeemopstellingen, (2009) Alta Mira, Netherlands.

Botschaften aus dem indigenen Feld Ritualle Elemente und Zeremonien in Systemaufstellungen (2009) Carl-Auer, Germany.

Feather Medicine, Walking in Shoshone Dreamtime: A Family System Constellation, (2004) Llumina Press, (2016) Create Space Independent Publishing Platform.

Contributing Writer: Praxis der systemaufstellung: Die Welt der Aufstellung, Familien und andere soziale Systeme. (2010) Carl Auer Verlag, Heidelberg, Germany.

Contributing Writer: Unten rum...Die Scham ist nicht vorbei: Claudia Haarman, (2008) Orlanda Frauenverlag GmbH, Berlin,.

Interviewed in: Mütter sind auch Menschen: Mütter und Töchter begegnen sich neu: Claudia Haarmann, Innenwelt Verlag GmbH, Köln, Germany, (2005)

Resources:

All My Relations Constellations website: www.allmyrelationsconstellations.com

International Directory of Systems Constellation Facilitators: https://www.talentmanager.pt/en/internacional-directory/#1436785481500-45dc51c5-13de

International Systems Constellation Association: https://isca-network.org/register/

Hellinger Institute of DC: https://www.hellingerdc.com/product-category/books/

The Knowing Field, International Journal on Systemic Constellations in English: https://www.theknowingfield.com

Real Academy: Resources for Embodied Ancestral Learning: https://realacademy.net/ref/sboring